EMERGENCY NUMBERS

Family Doctor: _____ After Hours: _____

_____ _____

_____ _____

_____ _____

Gynecologist: _____ _____

_____ _____

Pediatrician: _____ _____

_____ _____

_____ _____

Dentist: _____ _____

_____ _____

_____ _____

Pharmacist: _____ _____

_____ _____

_____ _____

Hospital Emergency Room _____

Ambulance _____

Poison Control Center _____

Police _____

Fire _____

Other _____

OUR FAMILY MEDICAL RECORD BOOK

Robert O. Patterson

POPLAR BOOKS

Copyright © 1982 by Poplar Books,
a Division of Book Sales, Inc.,
110 Enterprise Avenue, Secaucus, N.J. 07094

Designed by Barbara Levine

Manufactured in the United States of America

ISBN 0-89009-599-X

0 9 8 7 6 5 4 3 2 1

TABLE OF CONTENTS

Chapter One

How To
Use This Book

One of the most important elements in obtaining good medical and health care for your family is to keep good records of past problems and care that your family has received. That's the main purpose of this book: to provide a convenient place to record diagnoses and treatments which each member of the family receives throughout your lives together. And when the children grow up and leave home to start families of their own, they can take copies of their childhood and adolescent medical and health records with them — a major advantage when starting a new family.

There is space in this volume to record the detailed health and medical records of a father and mother and up to eight children. In addition, there is space for health summaries of all four grandparents, aunts and uncles and sisters and brothers of the father and mother. This gives an overview of the familial health profile which is invaluable for physicians monitoring pregnancies or treating health problems of individual family members.

RECORDS OF RELATIVES

Because there are a number of hereditary or family-related health conditions which may be recessive through a generation or two, it is important that the health and medical records — at least in broad outline — be known for members of the immediate family. That includes the parents of both the father and mother (grandparents), all of the aunts and uncles, and the sisters and brothers of the father and mother of the family using this book as a record and reference.

It isn't necessary to talk to each relative in person; usually the health record of most are known to the grandparents. If the grandparents have died, it may be necessary to ask a few questions of each of the aunts and uncles in order to record a complete family health profile. Experience has shown that most people are eager to assist in such a project, once it is explained to them. In fact, many start their own comprehensive records as a result of contributing to a relative's project.

IMMEDIATE FAMILY RECORDS

One of the most difficult parts of keeping an accurate record of health and medical treatment is the specialized "jargon" which is spoken by the average physician. Statements such as, "Your son has a mild case of rhinitis from a virus infection," might not mean to the average parent, "Your son has a common cold with inflamed nasal tissues." Because such jargon is often difficult to translate, we have provided a "Quick Dictionary of Conditions, Tests and Treatments."

This glossary of the terms most commonly used by physicians will enable you to interpret what your doctor says, what the tests reveal, and what is involved in the treatment he proposes. Don't ever be reluctant to ask the doctor for a full explanation of his or her diagnosis. An informed patient is a better patient than a patient who has no idea of what the physician said.

A NEW DOCTOR

Because families today move frequently, having a family doctor for most of a lifetime is an exception. As a result, medical records for most people tend to be scattered around among a great number of dcotors: family doctors, pediatricians, gynecologists, etc. The same thing is true of dental records.

By having a complete health and medical record for each member of the family, you will be able to inform new doctors of the important medical occurances which form the basis of your medical history. It is also recommended that medical records be transferred from the old doctor or dentist to the new one whenever a change is made, for any reason.

Most doctors today destroy inactive medical records after a certain period of time, which would make it impossible years later to go back and locate the exact diagnosis and treatment prescribed. The careful recording of information in this book will help, but it is a good idea to have your old doctor send your records to your new doctor. Most physicians will do this as a matter of course. Some will request a small fee for the administrative costs.

EMERGENCIES

There is a section on some of the common emergencies which occur in the family — particularly when there are children. In addition, at the front of this book is a space to list all of the emergency telephone numbers of the physicians, dentists and emergency services which could be required in case of an injury or illness which strikes suddenly.

It is also a good precaution to have the same type of list fastened to the bottom of the telephone base with plastic tape, so it is there in an emergency.

In many communities, pharmacists have emergency numbers; in others, they take turns in answering calls for emergency prescriptions. You can usually find this number by asking your local pharmacist, or by asking your doctor's receptionist.

PUT IT DOWN IN WRITING

How many times have you been at the doctor's office and have left without remembering a question which you wanted to ask? It happens frequently, but it won't if you have a list of the questions you want to ask made up in advance, and take the paper with you into the doctor's office. Then you can refer to it, and each of the questions will be answered.

Conversely, if you feel you don't understand what the doctor has said, ask him to write his diagnosis or the treatment down on a piece of paper so you "can put it in your home medical record." Few doctors object to this, in fact, most know that the paitent frequently fails to understand fully because of the tensions and nervousness associated with a doctor visit.

Immediately after getting home, get out this book and enter the information in the proper pages. A comprehensive record of each visit will be invaluable to you in the future.

Chapter Two

Hereditary and Congenital Conditions

Many younger people worry about the chances that their children, particularly the first child, will have birth defects, either from hereditary or from a mishap during conception or pregnancy. While it is true that some form of birth defect — from serious to inconsequential — may be found in one of every 16 babies born, a large portion of those are avoidable by modern tests and heredity matching procedures.

Defects are not spread evenly over the entire population. For example, sickle cell anemia is found primarily among blacks. Tay-Sachs disease is found primarily among Jews. Older women, past 40, have a majority of the children suffering from Down's syndrome (mongolism).

The following are the more common birth defects, listed primarily to assure a younger married couple that many of these can be detected long before birth.

THE EFFECTS OF DRUGS

One doctor tells her patients that even an aspirin should not be taken during pregnancy without getting her permission first. She says this dictatorial statement is designed to bring to her patient's attention the fact that any drug should be suspect while the baby is gestating in the mother.

Females whose mothers took a drug called DES (diethylstilbesterol) have a tendency toward cancer of the reproductive organs. Many remember the children born of mothers who had been given thalidomide by their doctors, children often without arms or legs.

Today's guiding principle is the less drugs the better during pregnancy. And because most of the damage done by drugs is during the first few days or weeks of pregnancy, many doctors advise women who are thinking of pregnancy or who think they might be pregnant to refrain from taking any drug or medicine unless prescribed by their doctors — who have been informed that the women think they may be pregnant.

Heroin, one of the most addictive drugs, has not been found to produce defects in gestating babies, but children carried by an addicted mother will be born with that addiction — transmitted through the mother's system to the unborn child.

PREVENTING BIRTH DEFECTS

Scientists today know far more about what causes birth defects than ever before, and that knowledge is being added to each day. Heredity and medical history are two clues that they use to determine the risk of birth defects. By recording medical histories of grandparents, aunts, uncles and brothers and sisters, by recording in detail your own and your children's medical histories, you provide doctors with much of the detail necessary to head off birth defects.

In addition, there are some precautions which you can take yourself. Don't have children too early or too late. The ideal time for childbirth is from 20 years old to 35 years old. Before 18 and after 40 is increasing the chances of having defective babies.

That doesn't only apply to mothers. The father should be under 45 for the best possible odds against birth defects. But an older father is not as big a risk as an older mother.

Don't have your children too fast. The ideal spacing between pregnancies should be at least two years (between the end of one and the beginning of another). Research has shown that children born too soon after another often have lower intelligence than first borns or children who have been properly spaced.

The pregnant woman should take good care of herself. Good food, but not so much that she becomes overweight beyond the doctor's recommended increases, exercise, stopping smoking, not using drugs or medicines except prescribed by the doctor, good prenatal care, including dietary supplements of minerals and vitamins, avoidance of X-ray or other radiation, care to avoid premature birth and delivery at a good, well-equipped hospital — all of these are positive steps in insuring a healthy child.

If you are black, you should ask for a test for sickle cell trait, both for yourself and your husband. The same thing applies for Tay-Sachs disease if you and your husband are Jewish. It takes two carriers of the specific gene for each of these conditions to produce a child with the defect. Even then, the odds are even that the child will not have the condition. (If tests are performed during pregnancy, such defects can be determined early and the pregnancy terminated if they exist.)

If the mother has a negative Rh factor, special care is required. Under certain circumstances, a vaccine is given after the birth of a child to insure that an Rh factor difference between mother and father will not affect a second child if the first is born without difficulty.

An important factor is genetic counseling. This requires having the medical histories of relatives of each marriage partner as far back as possible, so the counselor, usually associated with a hospital or family planning clinic, can develop some assumptions about the amount of birth defects within the two familial strains. Modern tests can determine the presence of a number of hereditary precursors of certain defects, such as sickle cell anemia, Tay-Sachs disease and hemophilia.

BIRTHMARKS

Birthmarks are a congenital defect which are generally caused by a malformation of blood vessel growth in a localized area. Some are small (strawberry marks) and some are large (port wine stains). The smaller strawberry marks will often disappear by themselves within the first few years of life, even though they appear to grow larger at first. Port wine stains may be covered by cosmetics, but most attempts to remove them, including freezing, tattooing, dermabrasion and radiation, have been unsuccessful overall.

Moles are another type of birthmark, although not as noticeable. Moles often disappear with age, but frequently not for 20 years or so. If a mole is in an unsightly place, it can be surgically removed by a doctor.

CEREBRAL PALSY

Cerebral palsy is considered as one of a series of defects due to brain damage of the infant before or during birth. Other defects are epilepsy, learning disorders and mental retardation. It is generally not inherited. German measles in the mother during the first part of pregnancy can be a major cause. Rh disease (an Rh negative mother who carries an Rh positive baby and builds up antibodies to the child's blood) may be a cause. So can diabetes in the mother, and premature babies have a greater percentage of palsy than normal term children.

Parents usually discover the problem because of differences in the way the child develops. It is usually detected early in life. While there is no cure, many cerebral palsy victims can be trained to overcome the effects of the problem which include motor and speech difficulties. A large percentage are also mentally retarded, but that retardation can vary from very slight to fairly severe. Tests can usually determine the degree fairly early.

CLEFT LIP OR PALATE

A birth defect which was once a tragedy for the child and family, both cleft lip and cleft palate can now be treated surgically by from three weeks to three months. For the child with a cleft palate and difficulty feeding, special prosthetic inserts may be used until time for the operation. Further operations, particularly with cleft lips, may be necessary during the child's growth, in order to minimize scarring and the tightening sometimes caused by normal growth stresses.

Modern methods leave most children having such defects with minimal visual and speech effects. Many children with cleft palates, however, show other birth defects, such as deformed limbs.

4

CLUBFOOT

Clubfoot is usually a positional problem of the fetus. It once was a child and adult crippler, but today modern surgical techniques are able to restore normal function to a vast majority of such cases. Clubfoot is the most common of all birth defects, with some research indicating that one child in 300 is born with one or both feet deformed. Boys have one type more frequently than girls, but both suffer from the condition. Manipulation and support, such as casts or bandaging, may cure about half of the cases. Surgery is required on the rest, but in almost every case, the condition can be corrected.

It sometimes appears again later in life, but surgery is effective then, too.

CYSTIC FIBROSIS

Cystic Fibrosis is a chronic lung problem which is inherited from parents with recessive genes for the condition. An abnormally sticky mucus is formed in the child's lungs which causes coughing, difficulty in breathing, little resistance to colds — which become dangerous to the cystic fibrosis victim — and difficulties in digestion or absorbtion of food.

Modern medical management of the condition has improved, with most children reaching adulthood. Early detection is essential, and if a child in the first months of life seems to have difficulty breathing or coughs a lot, the doctor should make skin tests which indicate the condition.

DIABETES

Diabetes in children is inherited, and it usually does not appear until the child is between 8 and 12 years old. It may also appear in middle age, or in old age. For children with the condition, it is important that they be under a doctor's care, that they learn to observe a special diet, and that they learn the importance of medication (either injected or ingested).

Diabetes is a metabolic condition which prevents the proper handling of sugars by the system. This creates a great number of side effects which can cause death if not controlled. Modern medical care, however, enables the average child with diabetes to live a full, healthy life.

Unfortunately, outside of family histories, there is no test which can determine if the parents are carriers of the gene which produces diabetes.

HEMOPHILIA

Hemophilia, the "bleeding disease," is an inherited condition passed on by mothers to their sons. It is a lack of an anti-clotting factor in the blood of the sufferer. Today, special management of the victim, including injections of a concentrate of the special factor (which is still very expensive and scarce) can stop bleeding episodes quickly.

While a child is encouraged to live a normal life, care must be exercised to overcome any after-effects of injuries such as falls, bruises and cuts which would be routine in a normal child. Hopefully, the anti-clotting factor will be synthesized cheaply and will be available to all. Family history is the only indicator of whether a child may be born with hemophilia.

HYDROCEPHALUS

Hydrocephalus (roughly translated as "water on the brain") is a condition which affects some one out of 500 newborns. It is what is called a multi-factorial condition; some cases are clearly hereditary, some are congenital (formed during pregnancy); inflammations or injury can also be causes. A goodly number of cases occur in conjunction with spina bifida.

Normally a child produces from three to five ounces per day of cerebrospinal fluid which bathes the brain, carrying minerals, proteins and other nutrients. The excess flows down the spinal cord and is finally absorbed into the blood stream. When the normal vents from the brain are closed, hydrocephalus occurs, with the pressure of newly forming fluid creating pressure on the skull and the brain itself.

A large number of children spontaneously recover. Surgery is recommended for others. In recent years, physicians have been able to determine hydrocephalus in unborn babies with the aid of ultrasonic examination and have actually relieved the pressure by draining the skull without removing the baby from the mother. Prolonged pressure can cause retardation of intelligence.

PHENYLKETONURIA (PKU)

Phenylketonuria is a hereditary defect of metabolism which makes it difficult or impossible for the child to convert a protein factor called phenylalamine into a form which can be utilized by the body. Milk, which contains large amounts of phenylalamine, creates surpluses of this chemical in the child's body, which spill over into the bloodstream where it affects the brain tissue. A special diet is required for such children.

A blood test can tell if the mother is a carrier of the defective gene which causes the condition.

Rh DISEASE

A woman with a negative Rh factor (so named because it was discovered in tests of rhesus monkeys) who marries a man with an Rh positive blood (the most common kind, with 94% of blacks and 85% of whites having this type) could have serious problems in pregnancy.

The Rh negative women react to the baby's Rh positive blood as if it was an invading virus. Because there is little transfer of the child's blood to the mother until actual childbirth, the first baby with the different blood type is usually born without difficulty. However, the mother's body then builds antibodies against that type of blood, so a second or third child with Rh positive blood would be attacked by these antibodies, causing conditions from mild anemia to death of the fetus by the sixth or seventh month.

An Rh positive mother will not react against an Rh negative child. Two Rh negative people will have no problems with their children's Rh factors. It is only when the mother is Rh negative and the father is Rh positive that the problem can occur.

Blood tests quickly determine if the mother has the negative factor. Transfusions have been developed to replace the baby's positive blood in the womb. But the biggest advance has been an Rh vaccine which can be given to the women to prevent them from developing the antibodies.

SICKLE CELL ANEMIA

A hereditary disease, affecting primarily blacks, this condition causes the blood cells to assume abnormal shapes, which do not adequately carry oxygen to the cells of the body. The abnormal blood cells also clump and cause blood clots which clog arteries and veins and often result in the death of surrounding tissue. It is a painful and difficult condition, and unless special care is taken with the victim, life may be severely shortened.

Blood tests of prospective parents determine if the defective gene exists, and blood test of the unborn baby will indicate if the condition exists in the child. There is no cure for sickle cell anemia, but management techniques have improved to the point where a substantial number of victims can lead relatively normal lives.

SPINA BIFIDA

Spina bifida is a condition which has multi-factorial causes, both hereditary and pre-natal. It involves a deformation of the spinal column, which in its least severe form is incomplete formation of several of the spinal vertebrae. The next most serious form is an abnormality large enough so some of the spinal nerve roots and spinal fluid are forced through the bony protection of the spine to form a sac enclosed by the spinal membrane (meninges). The most serious is when this sac actually contains part of the vital spinal cord.

There is no advance test which will determine if a child will have spina bifida, however, surgical and management techniques improve a child's chance for a productive life.

TAY-SACHS DISEASE

Tay-Sachs disease is a hereditary condition which affects primarily Jews whose ancestry traces to a certain section of Eastern Europe. Babies with the disease seem perfectly normal at birth, but soon their development slows down. The child loses motor functions, becomes blind and deaf and gradually becomes mentally retarded. Most such children die before their fourth year of life.

Laboratory tests to determine if parents are carriers of the disease have been developed. It takes the defective gene in both parents to produce a baby with the condition. If only one has the condition, a child may be a carrier, but will not have the disease.

6

Despite all of the terrible conditions listed above, there are a vast majority of children born with no major birth defects at all. When heredity is the cause, there is usually some test today which will provide prospective parents with an indication of the possibility of defects in their children. And in many cases, tests are available which will tell if the child has a major birth defect far in advance of delivery, so a pregnancy can be safely terminated if the child will be born with major abnormalities.

Chapter Three ————

Environmental and Allergic Conditions

The environment around us can be filled with both overt and subtle dangers. Everyone is well aware of the dangers of radiation, of pollution of streams and lakes, of fish with high mercury levels, with old houses that were painted with lead-containing paints, of chemical plants which develop carcinogens. But for many of us, there are other substances — harmless to most people — which cause pain, suffering and even disfigurement.

These are the allergens, the substances which create allergic attacks in susceptible individuals. Such things as plant pollen, cat or dog hairs, wool, certain foods, chemicals in soaps and common household products — can cause great distress in some people who are allergic to them.

ENVIRONMENTAL DANGERS

Let's look first at some of the things which exist in the environment which can endanger us all. Radiation is a major cause of cancer. It could come from nuclear material wastes improperly disposed of, from exposure to broadcast radiation of certain types of electronic equipment (early television sets and microwave ovens were implicated in such radiation), and overexposure to X-rays.

We are all continuously exposed to a certain level of radiation; normal "background" radiation is with us almost everywhere mankind is thickly settled. It is high doses or extended periods of lower dosage which causes the problems.

Another environmental problem is polluion of streams and lakes, of air and of the very food we eat. Pollution may take many forms, but some are so relatively new that it will be years before physicians know whether long term effects will be harmful or not. Waste dumping by manufacturers, emissions from combustion or chemical processes, and the disposal of solid wastes from the processes of civilization — can all be hazardous to health.

Pollution of food, both by nature and by man, can cause great health problems. High mercury levels in certain fish can be toxic to humans. Growth compounds given meat animals can poison or cause birth defects in humans. Insecticides can be absorbed by fruits and vegetables and affect man when the food is consumed.

WORKPLACE HAZARDS

There are a whole host of workplace diseases which have arisen over the past years. Asbestosis, a congestive and often carcogenic condition caused by inhallation of asbestos fibers, is not only common in asbestos miners and processing plant workers, but also in plasterers, plumbers and even residents of buildings which contain this product.

Coal miners suffer from "black lung," a debilitating disease caused by breathing coal dust over an extended period. Longterm smokers often suffer — although so do non-smokers — from emphasema, a non-reversible deterioration of the cellular structure of the lungs.

A vast range of chemicals, with new ones being discovered every day, cause health hazards for workers. Benzene, a chemical used in plastics manufacturing, has been indicted as a carcinogen.

KEEP A RECORD

One purpose of this book is to provide a place to record exposure to radiation, to chemicals, or to pollution of hazardous types. Many times this information is not available until long after the exposure, but even if you read about the dangers of some substance or condition to which you were exposed, making a record of it will give physicians in the future clues to problems you may have developed as a result. Often, too, materials which are believed to be safe are later discovered to be harmful. When this fact is publicized, you can then note your exposure or use.

IS YOUR CHILD ALLERGIC?

An atopic child is one who is prone to allergies. It is a hereditary condition in most cases, with a child of allergic parents far more likely to be atopic than a child whose parents have no allergies. An atopic child is one who, when exposed to allergens (substances which cause allergic reactions in certain people) develops "hay fever" or asthma.

There may be other allergies, as well. Allergies of the skin are well known, as are allergies caused by bites of insects — particularly bees, wasps and hornets. Even a non-atopic person can develop allergic reactions to certain allergens if exposed to large enough amounts over a long enough time.

FOOD ALLERGIES

One of the first allergic symptoms of food allergy to appear is vomiting, which, followed by diarrhea, is a frequent indication of an allergy to milk. (An intolerance to milk because of the lack of the special enzyme needed to digest milk is usually first indicated by colic, then vomiting and often constipation.)

Few children seem to be allergic to mother's milk. The problem is usually cow's milk.

Another common allergy is one to wheat products. This includes bread, any foods which contain wheat flour, cakes, most cookies and pasta. In children such an allergy is usually referred to as a cereal allergy, because it is usually linked to oats, rye, corn, barley and malt as well.

Babies may also be allergic to eggs, fruit, vegetables, meats, fish and shellfish and chocolate. Few babies are allergic to more than one or two major classes of substances, so a diet can be custom tailored to the specific problems the child has with foods.

One major silver lining in food allergies is that most children tend to grow out of them before puberty — often before reaching the age of seven or eight.

Some food allergies result in rashes forming, particularly hives. This is particularly true of chocolate and shellfish.

SKIN ALLERGIES

Atopic dermatitis (eczema) can begin at any age, but is often found in the first year of life. It is a rash which itches, and when scratched, becomes inflamed, oozes, crusts and often thickens. Interestingly, emotional upset generally seems to bring on or increase a number of allergies, and eczema is particularly suseptible to emotional causes. A baby who suffers from eczema will be less affected by the condition when protected, comfortable and coddled than when upset.

Diaper rash is probably the most common skin problem of babies. The skin under a diaper is often reddened and tender, particularly when plastic or rubber water (and air) proof pants are used over the diaper. It is caused by the irritating chemicals in urine and feces which leave the skin vulnerable to infection as well. There are a few simple rules. Keep the baby dry, and see the baby gets adequate liquids to drink, for low liquid intake results in concentrated urine which irritates more than dilute. Talcum powder can be used to keep the skin dry. Irritated skin can be hurried to heal with baby oil or a light coating of petroleum jelly. Don't use bleaches or harsh detergents in washing diapers. If detergents are used, rinse the diapers twice as thoroughly (use twice as much water) as an automatic machine usually provides. That means putting the diaper load (which should be washed separately from all other clothing and items) through the entire rinse cycle twice.

Diaper rash is really a form of contact dermatitis. This can also develop in sensitive babies from contact with chemicals or clothing. The most frequent chemical dermatitis in small children is soap and detergents, although paints and glues, fruit juices, insect sprays, perfumes, deodorants and shoe polish (dyes) are common causes. Obviously, most of these affect children older than infants.

Clothing which cause contact dermatitis in suseptible children can be leather, wool, nylon, rayon, rubber, or a perfectly innocuous fabric which is impregnated with a dye to which the child is allergic.

Hives are another manifestation of allergy. They may be caused by an allergy to food, drugs, infection, emotional upset, or any one of several other causes, including airborne materials, chemicals and paints, etc.

BITES

A common allergic reaction is that caused by bites of insects, with bees, wasps and hornets the most common offenders. But spiders, mites, fleas, sand fleas, bedbugs and other biting and burrowing insects can cause allergic reactions in a susceptible child. A normal reaction to a bite is pain, itching and a raised weal. An allergic reaction is generalized, such as overall swelling, itching or redness, which generally occurs about 15-20 minutes after the bite or sting. There may also be wheezing, vomiting, fainting and disorientation. Severe reaction may even produce coma and death.

Parents with susceptiblke children should rush them to the doctor or an emergency room. When susceptibility is known, however, a home emergency kit of adrenalin, antihistamines and other medications recommended by the physician should be kept on hand — and as the child grow older, carried in a pocket out-of-doors for self administration by the older child. Playmates and parents of playmates, school officials and teachers should be warned of the problem and the child's requirement for assistance to a physician.

BRONCHIAL ASTHMA

In a child, asthma — a general term used to described attacks of breathing difficulty, regardless of cause — is generally caused by reaction to specific allergens. It also tends to come in "spells," to be episodic. Many children who develop asthma during their first three years will grow out of the condition spontaneously by puberty.

Foods, drugs, pets, and colds are common causes of asthma attacks in younger children. Air pollution is also known to cause asthma attacks, and the only remedy for that is to remove the child from the area of pollution.

HAY FEVER

This is one of the most common allergies of adults, but is less common in children. Some doctors believe it is because hay fever is a gradual sensitization to specific allergens, usually plant pollens, over a period of time in a susceptible individual.

Hay fever is typically a condition of mucous membrane inflammation, including swelling and weeping of the eyes, dripping nose, sore throat, and often a wheezing breathing. Most of the symptoms can be confused with those of the common cold, but hay fever sufferers soon identify the specific pattern of their allergy. Antihistamines are useful in management of the condition.

IDENTIFICATION AND TREATMENT OF ALLERGIES

No parent should try to diagnose a child's reaction to irritants. A physician should identify if the child has an allergy, or is merely specifically responding to some local irritation which has no overall allergic affect. Diaper rash, which is an allergic reaction to specific irritants is not a general allergy. On the other hand, asthma or hives may indicate a deepseated allergy.

The same caution should be used for treatment. The physician should be consulted and the results of the treatment reported carefully. The first treatment for an allergy is not always successful. It takes time to determine the cause and to settle upon a regimen that will keep the child as comfortable as possible.

When food is the culprit, for example, doctors may have to use an elimination diet to determine which food is actually causing the problem. An elimination diet is one in which all food except a basic set, such as rice, tea, lamb, vegetables and gelatin desserts are withheld for a week. If improvement is noted, one food a week is added until symptoms of allergy again appear, then that food is placed on the prohibited list. While such a test takes time, it is the only reliable measurement of which foods cause allergy in the infant.

With other substances, "patch" tests may be required. These are also known as skin tests, for the skin is exposed to the materials suspected of being allergens by applying a patch, usually adhesive tape, containing the materials, directly to the skin. This also is a long process, but it isolates the specific substances which cause the symptoms in an allergic child.

Chapter Four
Food and
Nutritional Concerns

"You are what you eat," the wise man said, and that is still as true today as when early man came out of the cave to hunt for things to feed upon.

Nutrition is the cornerstone of good health. If the body is fed properly, it will be healthier. Although good eating habits alone won't prevent disease and injuries, a well-nourished body will have the maximum ability to fight off the effects of such assaults upon health. However, it must be remembered that good nutrition is only one of the cornerstones to good health. The others are exercise and rest. Particularly for children, the last two are equally as important as the first.

Good nutrition doesn't mean "fat." It has been a tradition in the Western world for parents and grandparents to believe a rollypolly, plump baby was healthier than a lean one. According to most of today's experts, " 'tain't necessarily so." By overfeeding an infant, these same experts believe that the doting parents are giving the child a tendency toward life-threatening obesity for the rest of its life.

What is good nutrition? It's different things at different times of life and for different sexes.

FEEDING YOUR BABY PROPERLY

There has been a great resurgence in breast feeding among today's mothers. Not only is the nutritional aspect of mother's milk now known, but the fact that it contains antibodies which will give the child a protection against a large number of common diseases and infections is understood by far more people than 30 or 40 years ago. While cow's milk is digested well by most babies, it does not have the same nutritional makeup as human milk. For those babies who cannot tolerate cow's milk, there are other (primarily soybean derivatives) formulas available, but these too suffer greatly in comparison with the mother's own milk.

Remember that children who are bottlefed, with either milk or formula, generally need an iron supplement. Prepared formulas are available with or without iron added. Cow's milk, however, is deficient in iron and should be supplemented by cereals, meats and vegetables — particularly spinach — to be sure the infant receives the amount needed.

STAGES OF A BABY'S EATING SKILLS

Almost all babies are born with a sucking ability which grows stronger as the days pass. But various other mechanical feeding abilities are developed gradually as the months pass. Of course, these are average figures, and an amazing number of babies will develop faster or slower than the average. These benchmarks in development, however, will give some guidance and hope to parents coping with baby's feeding patterns.

0 - 4 months	good suction; can drink juices after three or four weeks
4 - 5 months	tongue control develops, but food cannot be scooped from spoon
5 - 6 months	lip control develops, and child can drink from a cup held to the lips
6 - 9 months	more control; food can be removed from spoon; stops dribbling from cup
9 - 12 months	finger control develops; finger food can be held; food preferences develop; cup can be held but spilling occurs

12 - 15 months	-	assertive about food; throws food and eating utensils
15 - 18 months	-	manipulative skills improve; cup can be held steadily;
	-	spoon and even fork can be used
18 - 24 months	-	child can drink through a straw; fork is used more easily

How early can a baby be fed solid foods? Strained foods (baby foods) can be given from four to six weeks — sometimes earlier — but most nutritionists and pediatricians suggest that three to four months is the best age. Junior foods are handled well at from about six to nine months. After that, soft finger foods can be ingested without too much trouble. Cookies are a finger food that babies quickly learn to handle.

SUGAR, AN INSTINCTIVE FAVORITE

Some nutrition "experts" have proclaimed that the liking for and desire for sweets is a "learned" reaction, and if parents will merely see that children are not introduced to sugar containing foods, there will be no craving for such sweets. In reality, however, almost all animals like sugar and sweets from the time they are first tasted. The liking for sweet things is apparently an instinctive mechanism.

But sugar-laden foods (some dry breakfast cereals are more sugar than cereal grains) have ill effects on humans. Number one is the effect upon teeth. Cavities among sugar eaters is far higher than those in children whose sugar and sweets intake is limited. Another problem is a type of hypoglycemia (low blood sugar). Shortly after eating a substantial amount of sweets, the child exhibits the irritability, lack of concentration and irrationality that is typical of low blood sugar.

A major danger with sweets, however, is not a direct one. It is the likelihood that the child will fill up on sweets rather than eat a balanced diet. From a nutritional standpoint, this is the major cause for concern.

THE FOUR FOOD GROUPS

Whether a child or an adult, good nutrition demands that a variety of foods be eaten. The reason is that humans are omnivores (eating both animal and vegetable foods). A major part of the nutritional demands of the body must be met through eating a balanced diet.

To get such a balanced diet, there are four food groups which contain all of the nutrients such as protein, carbohydrates, fats, vitamins and minerals that the human body requires for long term functioning at peak efficiency.

Dairy Group -This group includes milk — whole, low fat, skim; cheeses, including cottage cheese; butter and cultured milk products like yogurt.

Meat Group -This group includes all types of meat — beef, pork, lamb, veal, mutton, and poultry, fish and eggs. It also includes the substitutes for meats, including the legume family (peas, beans and lentils), which provide high protein value. Nuts are also included in this group, because of their high protein content. Protein is an essential building block for growth.

Vegetable-Fruit Group -This group includes just about all the fruits and vegetables. Especially important are the green, leafy vegetables (lettuce, spinach, etc.), the dark yellow vegetables (carrots, sweet potatoes), potatoes, the cabbage family (cabbage, cauliflower, brussels sprouts, broccoli, etc.), and all other vegetables — and the fruits: citrus fruits (oranges, grapefruits, tangerines, lemons, etc.), pit fruits (peaches, apricots, nectarines, etc.), pears and apples, the berries, etc.

Bread-Cereals Group -This group includes all breads and cereals, whether made from wheat, rye, oats, barley, rice, etc.

It is vital that children and adults include adequate amounts of each of the four groups in daily diets. The dairy group provides minerals and fats (which are necessary to good health); the meat group provides protein and the B vitamin family; the vegetable-fruit group vitamins (especially A and C), iron; and the bread-cereal group carbohydrates (food energy), protein and minerals.

SPECIAL NUTRITIONAL NEEDS

Vitamin D (usually added to milk), is necessary for good health. Vitamin D is manufactured by the body from exposure to the sun, but growing children need adequate supplies of that vitamin and adults who work indoors all day also need additional supplies.

Girls past puberty and adult women through to menopause require additional iron supplies due to the monthly discharge of iron-containing blood during menstruation. Such iron must be obtained by either a high iron diet (liver, spinach, dried fruit, enriched bread, etc.), or by iron supplenents.

If you live away from the sea (or don't like a seafood diet), iodized salt is advisable to prevent thyroid gland problems (goiter).

If you or anyone in your family suffers from anemia, an adequate supply of protein should be eaten (meats, legumes, bread, dairy products, etc.), and since much anemia — particularly among women — is iron deficiency related, the iron content of the diet should be increased.

VITAMINS AND MINERALS: ARE THEY NECESSARY?

Calcium and phosphorus are required to provide a supply of building and repair material for the bones. Growing children should get adequate supplies of calcium in the diet. This usually is accomplished by providing plenty of milk to drink. Skim and low fat milks have approximately the same amount of calcium as whole milk, and in some cases, even more.

Dairies often reinforce low fat milks with additional milk solids, including calcium-containing compounds. Skim milk has had all of the fat taken out; low fat has been reduced from whole milk's average 3.5% butterfat to either 1% or 2%. It is necessary to carefully check the carton or other milk container to determine which of the low fat concentrations you have obtained. Despite what some people believe, low fat milks are not extremely low in calories. They rest somewhere between the calories of whole milk (160-170 calories per 8 ounces) and skim milk (80 calories per 8 ounces). Low fat milk is generally about 110 calories to 125 calories per 8 ounces. (American beer is approximately 95 to 100 calories per 8 ounces).

B vitamins are vital for good health of blood and tissues. Vitamin C is required for skin and muscles. Vitamin A is needed for good vision, particularly night vision. Vitamin D is necessary for healthy hair and body organs.

Iron is required for blood manufacture in the body, and for the ability of the blood to carry oxygen throughout the tissues.

If everyone in the family is getting a well balanced diet, there is no need for additional vitamin or mineral supplements. But, in most families, meals are missed, junk food is eaten, diets are heavy in some nutrients and not in others, etc. For that reason, some specialists in nutrition advise taking a multivitamin preparation (liquid or tablets/capsules) with minerals each day. The concept is one of prevention; if the diet lacks the adequate vitamin or mineral, the supplement will provide it. What isn't used is generally discarded as waste.

A caution: Oil soluble vitamins, particularly Vitamins A and D, are not entirely excreted by the body if excessive doses are taken. Some is deposited with fat in the cells, and can be harmful in large concentrations in the tissues. (The amounts found in the average one tablet per day vitamin supplements are not large enough to cause problems.)

The use of specially colored and shaped children's vitamins is discouraged by many pediatricians who feel that the children will perceive them as candy and take far too great a dosage if the opportunity arises. Vitamins, as with any medicine, should be stored out of reach of small children, and older children should be well cautioned not to experiment with such supplements.

Chapter Five —————————————————
Childhood Injuries and Emergencies

Your child is sick or injured. What should you do?

The first thing is not to panic. More harm has been done by a panicked parent than by one who takes a moment to think clearly of what to do.

RECOGNIZING ILLNESS

It is surprising to new parents, but it takes some time to determine whether the infant is ill. Not all babies nor children show the same signs of illness. One child will run a raging fever over a slight cold; another may show only a slight rise for serious illness. Another child will get a white, pinched look, some children just get lethargic, or perhaps irritable and cranky. The new parent soon gets to know the specific signs in his or her own child.

A child has been out running and playing with other children and comes into the house red-faced (or pale), panting and seemingly weak. Quick, a hand on the forehead; yes, elevated temperature. Now the thermometer. Yes, the child's temperature is up two or three degrees. Should the child be taken immediately to the doctor of hospital emergency room? No. Wait a few minutes. Many children will gain elevated temperatures just by exerting strenuously. If that's the cause, it will go down again quickly, usually within a few minutes of rest and a drink of fluid. The flushing or pallor will also disappear rapidly, and the child will probably wonder what all the fuss was about.

While a few minutes won't make much difference in the course of an illness, it is important to be able to recognize when a child is ill. In the case of infants under four months, this is especially important. Any illness in a baby that young should result in a visit to the doctor. Small infants have less resistances to such infections as the common cold, particularly those that are exclusively bottle fed. Infants who are breast fed receive antibodies from the mother's milk which help head off viral and bacterial infections.

Of course, extreme symptoms, such as coma, convulsions, repetitive vomiting, delirium, etc., are sure indications of severe illness. It must be noted that some children have convulsions whenever their temperature rises above a certain level. Parents of such children will soon be informed by their doctors of this tendency and will be advised of measures to take when it occurs.

Whenever extreme symptoms appear, the child should be taken immediately to the doctor or to a hospital emergency room. In some localities, where a hospital is some distance away, there may be a local ambulance or fire/police emergency team which can respond rapidly to such emergencies.

EMERGENCY NUMBERS

Keep a list of emergency telephone numbers in several places. One is at the front of this book. Another is inside the medicine cabinet door. Another is on the base of the telephone. Few parents are calm enough in an emergency to begin a search through telephone books for those vital telephone numbers.

What numbers should you have:

• **The hospital emergency room number.** If you live within reasonable distance from a hospital (up to 5 miles away in the suburbs, 10 miles away in the country, or 2 miles in the city), this is the first place to call for advice in cases of injury or extreme symptoms of illness. The call should be made before the child is taken there, because there are often procedures which they can suggest which will alleviate pain, reduce the threat to life or stabilize the child's condition. This applies equally to an adult who is injured or who exhibits extreme symptoms such as those above, or of chest pains, choking or strangulation, etc.

• **The family doctor.** In many areas, the family doctor is nearer than the nearest hospital. In that case, it might be best to try the doctor first, particularly during office hours. In cases where there appears to be a life threatening or crippling danger, if an *immediate* response is not obtained (an answering service answers, for example, or the doctor is out), call the next emergency number at once.

• **The pediatician.** If it is a child who is injured or ill, the family pediatrician may be the first one called. If, however, there appears to be a life threatening or crippling danger, and an immediate response is not obtained, call the next emergency number.

• **Poison control center.** In most sections of the country there is a poison control center where immediate identification of common household poisons are made by phone and advice is given on what to do to assist the victim. It is vital to determine quickly just what a child ingested; an adult is usually able to indicate the suspected substance. The poison control center needs the information: the name of the rat poison, the name of the drug (by law typed on the prescription label), the name of the cleaning solution, etc. Your local pharmacist or family doctor or pediatrician can supply the number of the poison control center to call.

• **Ambulance service.** In cases where an automobile is not available, or the parent is too distraught to drive, an ambulance service may be the best solution for taking an injured or seriously ill child or adult to the nearest hospital. In most communities, ambulance personnel are trained in medical emergencies and can provide an on-the-spot emergency service.

• **Emergency teams.** Many police, sheriff's departments and fire departments have special emergency medical teams on standby to serve the community. These personnel are trained and equipped in life-saving methods and usually respond rapidly to emergency calls through the department's emergency number.

• **Family doctor's backup.** Many general practitioners have colleagues who serve as emergency backup when the doctor is on an emergency, out of town, etc. The name(s) should be obtained from the doctor's office staff.

• **Hospital general number.** If the emergency room number is busy, the hospital general switchboard can usually put an emergency call directly through to the emergency room.

IMMUNIZATION

Steady progress has been made in eradicating childhood diseases. Polio and measles are among the most recent to have changed from often epidemic proportions to the point where some younger pediatricians have never seen a case of polio and only an occasional case of measles. Scientists are hard at work developing vaccines for other diseases, and eventually most of yesterday's common illnesses of children will be extinct.

Nevertheless, a few cases of even polio and measles still are found — mostly because parents resisting having their children immunized because, "It's unnecessary, those diseases just don't exist anymore." Unfortunately those diseases do exist, either in carriers, in tourists or immigrants from other areas where the diseases still flourish, and even in some animals or insects.

Immunizations are vital parts of today's health programs. Many school systems will not allow a child to attend unless the required immunizations are obtained. The level of risk for most immunizations is so low as to be statistically unimportant. Even where there is a risk factor, however, the odds are still better for the child to be immunized than to risk developing most diseases, where the risk factor is substantially greater.

CUTS, SCRAPES AND BRUISES

The usual injury to a child is a scrape or bruise, with occasional cuts thrown in to create parental anxiety. In the vast majority of the injuries of childhood, the application of a bit of tender loving care, some antiseptic solution or spray, and an adhesive bandage is all that's necessary to send the child on its way.

Occasionally, however, there are more serious injuries: A bone is broken (or a break is suspected), the child is struck or falls on its head and either loses consciousness or acts "funny" afterwards, a cut is deep and will not stop bleeding. What do you do?

If a bone is broken or a break is suspected, call your doctor immediately. In cases of an arm or leg break, cradle the limb gently but securely so it cannot move and create more damage than already done. The cradling is usually done by a "splint," which can be made by using a rolled newspaper and tying the limb securely, but lightly at several points along its length. The immediate pain will diminish as the limb is supported. If the doctor can't be reached, phone and prepare the emergency room of the local hospital for your arrival with the child. Then, transport the child as quickly as possible.

If it is a compound fracture (the bone protrudes through the skin), which is less likely with smaller children, take care not to attempt to straighten the limb, but support it in the broken position. Start for the hospital at once. Use a clean compress against the wound to prevent bleeding.

If the child is struck or falls on its head, and there is evidence of a large bump or an indentation, or if the eyes seem "glassy," get the child to your doctor or to the hospital emergency room. Do not let the child "sleep it off." A concussion (bruising of the brain tissue) may have occured, and sleeping may permit the damage to increase. If there has been any loss of consciousness from the blow or fall, even if there is no symptom of dizziness or confusion, take the child to the doctor or hospital at once. When transporting the child, keep it lying down, and jostle as little as possible.

Sprains are merely tissue injuries. They are usually difficult to distinguish from fractures, however, particularly in small children. There is usually swelling, often discoloration, tenderness and pain upon movement. These symptoms could also exist with a fracture, particularly the type known as a "green stick" fracture, where the bone does not completely break in two, but develops small lengthwise splits. To be on the safe side, take the child to the doctor or to the hospital emergency room for X-rays to determine if there is a break.

Scrapes and bruises are the most common injuries of childhood. Under normal circumstances, neither of them has any long-term consequences. If the scrape has some embedded debris, from a fall on gravel, for example, clean it out before bandaging. Use an antiseptic solution, a spray or an ointment to prevent infection. There are a wide variety of these in drugstores and one or two should be in every home medicine cabinet for emergency use. After applying the antiseptic, bandage the scrape with a prepared adhesive bandage (Band-Aid), or with a pad of sterile gauze fastened with adhesive tape. If the scraped area is extensive (larger than 2" x 2") it is advisable to see a doctor. If the scraped area is on the face and is larger or deeper than a typical abrasion, it is wise to see a doctor to eliminate any worry about future scarring.

Bruises are more unpleasant looking than dangerous. A bruise is caused when a blow or other injury breaks small capillaries in and under the skin. Blood leaks from these little veins and disperses throughout the surrounding tissue. This causes the red to purple appearing bruise and often an accompanying swelling if the blood flow is large. Swelling can be reduced by alternating hot and cold compresses, but the appearance of the bruise will follow a typical path from red to purple to blackish, then brown and finally yellow as the body cleans up the spillage by itself.

BURNS

Of far more serious nature are burns. There are several ways a child can be burned: touching a hot object, spilling hot liquid, ignition of a flammable liquid, and sunburn.

Burns are classified by degree:

First degree burn: The skin is red and painful.

Second degree: Blisters develop.

Third degree: The skin is destroyed and the underlying tissue is involved.

Burns are difficult to classify initially, since it takes some time for blisters to form or for damaged skin to slough off and reveal the depth of the burn. In some cases, like touching a hot stove, the skin is lost quickly and the destruction of underlying tissue can be seen within a few minutes.

Minor burns can be treated at home by applying an ice pack to the injured area. The cold is both soothing and prevents formation of blisters. Sunburn can be treated with a sunburn lotion (not a sunburn prevention lotion), which contains a mild local anesthetic.

Serious burns should be immediately cared for by a doctor. Take the victim to the doctor or hospital emergency room at once.

POISONING

Poisoning is the third greatest cause of death in children. Prompt treatment is vital if poisoning is suspected. The most common types of poison taken by children are:

• **Household cleaning supplies,** which include lye (drain cleaners), ammonia, bleach and other chemicals, such as silverware dipping solutions and trisodium phosphate cleaners (wall and floor cleaners).

• **Household insect and rodent poisons,** including ant and roach sprays, rat and mouse poison baits, etc.

• **Garden supplies,** which include weed killers, insect poison sprays, and fertilizers.

• **Painting supplies,** including turpentine, mineral spirits, oxalic acid (wood bleach), etc.

• **Other common household chemicals,** including lighter fluids, kerosene for heaters, shoe polish, etc.

• **Medicine cabinet contents,** including prescription drugs; over-the-counter remedies, such as antihystaminies; cold remedies; rubbing alcohol; sunburn lotions, sleep aids; diet pills or capsules, etc. A particular over-the-counter remedy to keep out of the reach of children is aspirin. Each year, a number of children die from taking overdoses (as few as 10 to 12 tablets) of this common household remedy.

Attempt to determine what poison was taken and immediately phone your nearest poison control center. You should discover its phone number from your family doctor and keep it in the front of this book, as well as with other emergency numbers on the base of the telephone and the inside of the medicine cabinet door.

When the poison control center has given you the proper procedure and/or antidote, immediately phone your doctor or the hospital emergency room. If you do not have a car, phone the local ambulance service to take your child to the emergency room. Speed of reaction time is most important when you suspect poison.

Do not try home remedies yourself. Some poisons should be diluted by giving large quantities of liquids. Others should be vomited up. But if you pick the wrong treatment, you may cause more harm than good. The poison control center will give you the proper treatment to administer. Then getting your child into the hands of the experts as quickly as possible is vital.

DROWNING AND SUFFOCATION

Cessation of breathing can cause brain damage in from four to six minutes. The important thing is to get a child breathing again. For this, each parent should be aware of the basics of artificial respiration.

The American Red Cross recommends the following techniques:

1. Clear the mouth of any foreign matter with the middle finger of one hand. With the same finger, press the tongue forward.

2. Place the child in a face-down, head-down position with rear end elevated, and pat him firmly on the back with your free hand, continuing to hold the tongue forward with the other hand. This should help dislodge any foreign object in the air passage. This will also drain water from the lungs.

3. Place the child on his back and open his mouth by using the middle fingers of both hands to lift the lower jaw from beneath and behind so it "juts out."

4. Hold the jaw in that position using one hand.

5. Place your mouth over the child's mouth *and* nose, making a relatively leakproof seal, and breathe into the child with a smooth steady action until you observe the chest rise. As you start this action, move the free hand to the child's abdomen, between the navel and the ribs, and apply continuous moderate pressure to prevent the stomach from becoming filled with air.

6. When the lungs have been inflated, remove your lips from the child's mouth and nose and allow the lungs to empty through continued pressure on the abdomen.

Repeat this cycle, keeping one hand beneath the jaw and the other hand pressing on the abdomen at all times. Continue at a rate of about 20 cycles per minute. After every 20 cycles, you should rest long enough to take one deep breath. If at any time you feel resistance to your breathing into the child and the chest does not rise, repeat step 2, then quickly resume mouth-to-mouth breathing.

PUNCTURE WOUNDS

Children often step on pointed objects, or fall on them. These are usually dangerous only for the potential of tetanus bacteria being deposited in the tissues. Tetanus exists in dirt, and all wounds should be considered potentially dangerous.

That's why children should have tetanus immunizations as soon as they are able to go out and play outdoors. Booster shots can be given on a regular basis, and should be given if there is a serious puncture wound which penetrates the tissue beneath the skin.

ANIMAL BITES

Any animal bite should be reported to authorities at once. While there are only a relatively small number of rabid animals around domestic neighborhoods, some species, such as skunks and squirrels, carry rabies bacteria. If such an animal bites a local dog, that dog could become rabid.

If the animal which caused the bite can be caught and penned up for approximately two weeks, it will generally die during that time if it has rabies. The rather painful series of immunizations can then be given the child. If the animal cannot be found, most doctors will recommend the series of shots be given. Of course, if the animal passes the two-week confinement without any evidence of rabies, the child will not need the shots.

Chapter Six ————————————

Childhood Illnesses and How to Recognize Them

The major childhood illness in terms of numbers of times it will appear is the common cold. The cold is a virus disease, and doctors often refer to it as an APC infection (adenoidal-pharyngeal-conjunctival). This merely means that it affects the nose, throat and sometimes the eyes. There are more than 130 different varieties of viruses which have been identified as producing the symptoms of the "common cold."

Most parents cannot determine the differences between the common cold and influenza (flu). Both start in somewhat the same manner, both have somewhat the same symptoms, and both affect the same areas.

THE COMMON COLD

The onset of a cold is usually a slight ache, a headache, "scratchy" throat, a runny nose, and — in most younger children — a general irritability or "crankiness." Some children will have a reduced appetite, or may even refuse to eat at all. Others will have chills, and fever is quite common, particularly with younger children, whose temperature control mechanisms are not yet fully developed.

The average cold lasts about three to six days. The only remedies that doctors prescribe universally are rest, particularly bed rest, increased fluids, and aspirin to reduce the pain and fever. Most suggest cough medicines or throat losenges if there is a cough.

If the child has a fever, be sure to keep it in bed, particularly for one day beyond the time the fever ends. A relapse is quite common if the child is allowed to run and play vigorously the day after the fever has disappeared.

Don't worry about fever unless it exceeds the level that the doctor has established as a normal reaction to infection for your child. Fever is healing, but it does cause fatigue and dehydration. That's why it's so important to give the child lots of fluid constantly throughout the illness. The soothing effect of cool liquid against sore throat tissues makes it easy to get the child to accept fruit juices, lemonade, etc.

Most physicians do not recommend antibiotics for a cold. Antibiotics are not effective against a virus, and continued administering may just build up a toleance to their effects. On the other hand, if the child has a history of secondary infections from colds, such as middle ear infections, ulcerated tonsils, etc., the doctor may give antibiotics as a preventive measure. Leave it up to the doctor!

INFLUENZA

Influenza (flu) is also a virus disease, but of longer duration (8 to 10 days) and greater severity than the common cold.

Its onset is usually far more sudden than that of a cold, producing fatigue, a light-headed feeling, fever (up to five days), and sometimes nausea. There may also be a dry cough which develops within the first couple of days. Generally the child does not develop a runny nose.

Because of the length of the fever, it is especially important to guard against a relapse from allowing the child up and about too quickly. And, as with any fever, it is important to give lots of fluids. If the temperature of the patient exceeds that which the doctor has said is the child's normal reaction to infection, the doctor should be notified at once.

COMPLICATIONS OF COLDS AND FLU

The two major complications of both common cold and influenza are ear and sinus infections. If the child complains of pain in the ears, the doctor should make an examination at once. If the child complains about aching or pain in the temples above the eyes, or in the face next to the nose, the chances are that the sinuses have become infected. The doctor should examine the child and prescribe treatment.

Infants, especially during the first six months, are particularly susceptible to virus infections, especially those which have been bottle fed. Although it will create some problems, no adult or child with a cold, a runny nose, or a cough should be permitted to visit or come into contact with the child. Even the parents should be extremely careful during the time either has a cold.

Another complication is the croup, which is actually a type of laryngitis in smaller children and infants. Swelling of the throat causes a noisy breathing and a loud, shrill, barking cough. It is usually caused by the virus, or by bacteria which create an infection in an area inflamed by the virus.

Tonsillitis is another complication of a cold or the flu in children from two to eight years old. There are about 40 different strains of bacteria which take advantage of inflamation of the throat to settle into the tonsils and create an infection. About half of these are streptococcus germs, which also cause scarlet fever and rheumatic fever.

A sore throat and painful swallowing are usually good indicators of a tonsil infection. Using a tongue depressor, the swollen and usually translucently white or yellow tonsils can be seen easily. The child should be taken to the doctor for treatment.

Pneumonia is also an after effect of some colds or flu. It is caused by inflammation of the lungs, which causes fluid to collect in the bottom of the lungs. Once a potentially fatal disease, pneumonia today can usually be treated successfully with antibiotics. If the child has difficulty breathing or complains of pains in the chest upon breathing, it calls for a doctor's examination at once.

IMMUNIZATION AGAINST CHILDHOOD DISEASES

There are nine childhood diseases against which immunizations have proven successful. Since most school systems today demand that these immunizations be given, the diseases are gradually disappearing from the population. The influx of immigrants, the increased travel in other countries where such immunizations are not universal, however, make it vital for children to have the protection of initial immunizations, and — where required — the booster shots to keep the immunity intact.

Some immunizations are given by mouth, but most of them are in the form of shots, which are either given just under the skin (subcutaneously) or into the muscle tissue (intermuscularly).

DIPTHERIA

Diptheria is a bacterial (germ) disease which is highly contagious, affecting the throat. The symptoms are a sore throat, nausea, headache and a fever (100-104°F.). The throat swells and gray or dirty yellow colored patches appear. It is spread from person to person by airborne droplets from coughing or even speaking. In smaller children, the larynx is involved, and the child will lose its voice. Treatment is best administered in a hospital.

Immunization has been so effective that diptheria in the U.S. is a fairly rare occurance. However, it still exists in many parts of the world. Immunization is usually given in conjunction with a vaccine for whooping cough (pertussis) and lockjaw (tetanus), called D/T/P. Three injections are usually given, starting at one or two months of age and are spaced at about two month intervals. Boosters are usually given at 18 months and five years of age.

After a child is five years old, diptheria vaccine is usually given in combination with tetanus vaccine, with an additional booster given at the age of 15 and every 10 years after that. If traveling in an area where diptheria is prevalent, boosters should be given before traveling, as well.

GERMAN MEASLES (RUBELLA)

German measles, also called rubella and three-day measles, is a highly contagious virus disease, spread by airborne droplets from coughing or speaking. The symptoms are tiredness, headache, a sore throat with swollen neck glands, fever (up to about 101°F.), and joint pains about the third day of the illness. A rash may appear on the face and spread to the body, but many children have no rash at all with German measles. Complications in children with the disease are rare.

Note: Many doctors recommend immunization of women of childbearing age to prevent possible birth defects which are associated with rubella occuring in pregnant women. If such immunization is performed, contraception should be practiced for at least three to four months afterwards.

MEASLES (RUBEOLA)

Measles, also called rubeola, red measles, seven-day measles and 10-day measles, is a highly contagious virus disease with serious complications possible. Symptoms are fatigue, a headache, possible back pains, a dry cough, fever (up to 103-104°F. by the third day of illness), red, itchy eyes (and a sensitivity to light), and small white spots in the mouth, especially on the gums. About three days into the illness, a red, blotchy rash will appear on the face, usually around the hairline and behind the ears, and will spread over the face, down the neck and over the body to the arms and legs.

Complications are sore throats, ear infections and pneumonia caused by bacteria taking advantage of the virus weakened body. The most serious complication, fortunately quite rare, is the so-called measles encephalitis (infection of the brain), which is heralded by a stiff neck and convulsions. There may also be vomiting.

Immunization has made measles an endangered species, much to the rejoicing of U.S. parents. The vaccine may be administered by itself or with the vaccines for German measles and mumps in an M/M/R vaccine. It is a one-time vaccine, for immunity is granted with the one injection. It is usually given after the infant is nine months to one year old.

MUMPS (EPIDEMIC PAROTITIS)

One of the most common virus diseases of childhood is measles, which attacks the salivary glands at the back of the jaws. These glands, also called the parotid glands, and the sex glands (in adults) are the ones most commonly associated with mumps, although the pancreas and kidneys may also be affected by the disease. It is spread by airborne droplets by speech or coughing.

Symptoms of the disease are headache, earache, back pains, painful swelling of the parotid glands, and fever (100-104°F.) the day before the swelling appears and for a couple of days afterward. For some children, the taste (or even the thought) of sour or acid food or drink can cause pain.

Although children five to nine years old are the most common victims, immunizations are not advised for children by some doctors, who feel that symptoms are mild without major complications in pre-puberty. Others recommend that it be given at the age of one to three with measles and German measles in a M/M/R vaccine. Although vaccine or infection do not give permanent immunity, few adults have mumps if they contracted it or were vaccinated in their youth.

PARATYPHOID

Paratyphoid is a bacterial disease which resembles typhoid fever, even though it is related to the Salmonella family of gastric distress-causing organisms. There are two types, *Salmonella paratyphi A*, and type *B*. It is spread by food which is contaminated and poorly refrigerated.

Symptoms are fatigue, headache, fever (100-103°F.), with perhaps nausea and vomiting. Rose colored spots break out on the body of some children with the disease.

Immunization is usually given with the vaccine for typhoid fever. The vaccine is for typhoid and both the A and B varieties of paratyphoid (TAB vaccine). Some school districts require it for admittance, but many doctors recommend it only in areas where there are likely to be outbreaks of the diseases.

POLIOMYELITIS (INFANTILE PARALYSIS)

Poliomyelitis is also known as infantile paralysis, a contagious virus disease of the nervous system which was once of epidemic proportions in the U.S. There are four varieties, and contraction of one seems to provide immunity to all four. It was most prevalent in the summer and fall and affected children in the five to nine age group primarily, although adolescents and adults also contracted the disease. Immunization has now reduced the disease in the U.S. to a rare occurance, although refusal to have children immunized recently brought on a minor epidemic of polio.

Symptoms were a headache, nausea and vomiting, sore throat, stiff and painful neck and back, drowsiness and a fever of 100-101°F. These symptoms were the same for all four types: 1. Abortive (minor symptoms similar to a sore throat or cold, but giving complete immunity), 2. Nonparalytic (the symptoms of polio, but disappearing within a week or so with no apparent nervous system involvement). 3. Paralytic (weakness of muscles appears within 7 to 10 days, with partial or full paralysis resulting, particularly of lower extremities), and 4. Bulbar (within the first to third day of illness difficulty in swallowing, speaking and breathing occur). Bulbar polio was the type which required the iron lung to replace automatic respiration for the patient.

Immunization can be with either the Salk vaccine, which is a killed virus type injected into the subject, or with the Sabin variety, which is a live virus vaccine given by mouth — usually on a sugar cube. Most injections are of the trivalent type, that is, including vaccines for the main three types of polio viruses. They are usually given in three doses about two to three weeks apart in the first six months of life, then a single booster at 18 months and again at five years old.

The Sabin oral (OPV) vaccine is more potent, but has somewhat greater danger of side effects than the Salk injected (IPV) vaccine.

SMALLPOX (VARIOLA)

Smallpox, also called variola by public health experts, is a highly contagious virus infection, which has become so rare in this country and most of the world because of widespread immunization, that vaccination for it is no longer required in the U.S. One of the reasons for dropping vaccination was the danger of side effects on children.

Symptoms are a severe headache, chills and fever (101-104°F.), and in children, nausea, vomiting and convulsions. About the third or fourth day of the illness, a rash of small red, hard bumps like pimples appear on the face, arms and legs. After a few days the bumps become blisters filled with a clear fluid which then turns into pus and scabs over. The scabs fall off in three to four weeks, leaving deep pits which remain as permanent scars, particularly on the face.

Immunization is given by scratching the surface of the skin on a shoulder or hip and applying a drop of vaccine which contains live virus. A small, local reaction at the site the vaccination usually occurs. Vaccinations were originally given before a child entered school, at about five years old.

TYPHOID FEVER

This bacterial disease is usually transmitted by contaminated water, milk or food which has been handled by a carrier (someone who carries the disease without showing any symptoms). It is rare in most sections of the U.S.

Symptoms are fatigue, headache, loss of appetite, backache, nosebleeds, stomach cramps and a distended abdomen, and either constipation or diarrhea. Sometimes a sore throat accompanies early symptoms. There is a fever, which usually rises to 105°F. each day, dropping to about 100-101° at night. This occurs for about seven to ten days before dropping, but hangs on at lower temperatures for another seven to 10 days. In adults, the fever usually lasts about 21 days, but in children it can range from 10 to 21 days. Rose spots generally appear during the second week, primarily on the body. In some patients, there is delirium and a stuporous condition.

Immunization is generally given in conjunction with the vaccines for paratyphoid fevers A and B (TAB), when there is likelihood of an outbreak.

WHOOPING COUGH (PERTUSSIS)

Whooping cough, or pertussis, is a highly contagious bacterial disease with a high infant mortality rate, which is largely eradicated today. It generally affected children before the age of two. An airborne disease, it is spread by speaking, coughing or sneezing of victims.

Symptoms are listlessness, a runny nose, sneezing, loss of appetite, tearing of the eyes, and —

after about 10 to 14 days — the distinctive "whooping" cough, which can last for four to six weeks. The cough is distinctive because it is a spasmodic paroxym of deep rapid coughs, which cause the victim to suck in air noisily (the whoop) to keep from suffocating. Typically the face turns red or purple during coughing attacks.

Immunization is given in conjunction with diptheria and tetanus vaccines (DPT) at about two months of age. There are three injections, given two months apart, with a booster at 18 months and another booster at the age of five. Pertussis vaccine is then discontinued, although diptheria and tetanus injections are recommended at 10 year intervals throughout life.

NON-IMMUNIZABLE CHILDHOOD DISEASES

There are a number of common childhood diseases, spread by contact between children, which do not yet have available effective vaccines, although medical scientists are continually working on the problem. While most of these diseases confer immunity with a single infection, several have serious effects upon the child. A number are also found to affect adults more drastically than children.

CHICKENPOX (VARICELLA)

Chickenpox, or varicella, is a highly contagious virus disease which generally strikes most children between the ages of five to nine, although it may be contracted at any age. It is most common in the winter and spring. Spread by airborne droplets, the source of chickenpox is infected individuals who sneeze, cough and even breathe on others.

Symptoms are low-grade fever (99-101°F.), headache, back pains and loss of appetite. Small red spots appear almost at once on scalp or chest and back, later on abdomen and arms. After spots appear, blisters form in crops, at first filled with clear fluid then pus. Scabs form, itching severely until they peel off in 5 to 20 days.

INFECTIOUS MONONUCLEOSIS (GLANDULAR FEVER)

Mononucleosis, which used to be called glandular fever, is also known as mono. It is believed to be caused by a virus, and is also known as the "kissing disease," because it is not particularly contagious unless contact is made with nose and throat discharges of infected persons. It is primarily a disease of older children and young adults.

Symptoms are a sore throat lasting more than a week, swollen glands in the neck, nausea, chest pain, stiff neck, swollen eyelids, sometimes a rash and sometimes yellowish jaundice because of liver involvement. A general feeling of fatigue or lassitude is usually experienced after several days. A fever (100-101°F.) may last for weeks or months, rising and falling from morning to night. The overall weakness may persist for months.

MENINGITIS

Meningitis is an inflammation or infection of the meninges, the membrane which covers the brain and spinal cord. It may be caused by viruses, bacteria or fungi, but the epidemic type is caused by the meningococcal bacteria. Depending upon the area affected, meningitis is referred to as spinal or cerebral. The bacterial type is contagious, but not as much as other diseases such as chickenpox or measles.

The symptoms are a sudden headache, painfully stiff neck which will not let the child touch its chin to the chest, the child vomits, and there are chills and fever (103-105°F.). The child may also have convulsions or seems to be in a stupor. There may also be a fine rosy skin rash. Symptoms are difficult to identify in infants. Medical attention should be obtained as quickly as possible upon suspecting meningitis, for the course of the disease is extremely rapid.

RHEUMATIC FEVER

Rheumatic fever is a bacterial disease (streptococcus), which strikes primarily children between the ages of five and fifteen years. Its most serious consequence is heart disease. The disease is often associated with scarlet fever and "strep" throat, also caused by streptococcus bacteria. Rheumatic fever itself is not contagious, although the diseases from which it derives are.

Symptoms are ambigious. One child may have a severe onset of high fever (103-105° F.) with chills; a general achy "sick" feeling; swollen, red, painful joints, and a rapid or irregular pulse. Another might have a sore throat, after which a low-grade fever (99-101°F.) hangs on for several days, is pale and continually tired, and has various joint aches and nose bleeds.

ROSEOLA

Roseola is a common virus disease which usually affects children one to three years old. It generally occurs in the fall, winter and spring, and is often mistaken for German measles.

The symptoms are a high fever (103-105°F.) for three to four days, although the child may not seem to have any other symptoms of illness. As the fever abates, a rash appears, usually on the body. The rash, which is pink and slightly raised, will spread to the arms and neck but does not usually appear on the face or legs. It lasts about a day.

SCARLET FEVER (SCARLATINA)

Scarlet fever or scarlatina is a highly contagious streptococcal disease which is spread by contact with infected surfaces, airborne droplets from coughing, sneezing or even talking. It generally occurs in late winter and spring, and is most common among children five to eight years old, although older children and adults may easily contact it from the infected person. Its most serious complication is rheumatic fever.

Symptoms are a high fever (101-105°F.), an achy feeling, a headache, nausea and vomiting (the child may only vomit once), and a sore throat with swollen glands in the neck. There may be a general feeling of weakness or fatigue. About a day or two after the onset of the illness, a bright pink rash of small spots with a rough feel begins on the face and body and within two days covers most of the skin surface. There is often a whitish ring around the mouth. The rash will begin to fade in about five or six days, but the skin will peel for many days afterwards.

STREP THROAT (SEPTIC SORE THROAT)

Strep (streptococcus) sore throat, once called septic sore throat, is essentially a form of scarlet fever without the rash. It is caused by the same bacteria, and is highly contagious. It strikes children in the five to eight year age group most commonly, and may be difficult to differentiate from a viral sore throat, except by a throat culture. It is often spread by contaminated milk as well as direct contact.

Symptoms are almost exactly those of scarlet fever without the rash. There is fever (101-105°F.) occasionally with chills, achy feeling, headache, a sore throat with enlarged red tonsils and swollen glands in the neck, possible nausea, and a general feeling of weakness or fatigue.

Like scarlet fever, the main complication is rheumatic fever, although there have been cases of kidney involvement as well.

Chapter Seven————————————

How To Set Up
A Family Medical Plan

Somehow you haven't gotten around to finding a "family" doctor. You've just gotten married, or you've recently moved to another area, or you just haven't been sick, and don't think about having a doctor. Now's the time to select one, however: The baby is on the way, you or your spouse haven't been feeling up to par, or one of the children is looking and acting a bit under the weather. How do you go about it?

Believe it or not, a neighbor or a friend isn't too good a referral source to a doctor. Too often, people are more impressed by the doctor's personality — his or her bedside (or deskside) manner — and not by the actual level of service which is provided. Of course, if that friend or neighbor is a health professional — a nurse, medical technician, druggist, etc. — it's far more likely that the evaluation will be accurate.

PRIMARY CARE
What you should be looking for — in the jungle of all those specialists — is a family doctor. In the terms of the medical profession, that's a "primary care" physician. It's the type of physician who takes care of the medical needs of your family. If it is a routine checkup or just being sick, this is the physician who diagnoses what's wrong and prescribes treatment, sends you to the hospital for admission, or refers you to a specialist.

Some people want to go directly to the specialist. If they have a heart pain, they want a cardiologist (heart doctor). If they have a pain in the back, they want to go directly to an orthopedist (bone doctor). The problem with this is that the specialist is concerned with the specialty. What if the back problem was caused by something else — like kidney disease. Would the specialist recognize it? Probably the specialist would, but that would mean a visit to a nephrologist (kidney doctor).

By starting with a family doctor, you'll build up a medical history. The family physician can match up your present complaints with your history. And the family physician is more of a specialist on common illnesses and ailments, since that's what the average family doctor treats, day in and day out. If it's something that is outside his line of practice, such as eyesight, he'll refer you to the appropriate specialist, and that referral will be a far better one than any you can get from friends or by looking in the local yellow pages.

But what is a primary care physician?

It used to be that there were a large number of general practitioners (GPs) around — usually overworked and underpaid. But as young doctors finishing medical school looked at their futures, most of them decided that the hours and the income of the GP was not what they had in mind, and most of them went — and still go — into specialty practice.

That's not to say there aren't still general practitioners out there; there are. But many of them are older doctors. It's only been in the past decade or so that a new breed has sprung up: the family practitioner (FP).

Where the old GP used to start practice right after finishing internship, the new family practitioner gets a three-year residency in being a family doctor. That means specializing in the common illnesses and ailments that affect people everywhere. But there aren't a lot of FPs out there.

Many people go to the general internist. This is a physician who has focused upon such things as heart, lungs, gastrointestinal system, liver, kidneys, endocrine (glandular) system, etc.

An internist doesn't usually have training in pediatrics, orthopedics or obstetrics (pregnancy and childbirth), but usually has training in gynecology ("female" problems).

And more people today are selecting an osteopath for family physician. An osteopath is not an M.D., but receives the same type of medical training, internship and often residency as the M.D. In some states, notably California, an osteopath, upon completion of training, may select either the osteopath's O.D. or an M.D. In addition to general medical training the osteopath receives specialized training in manipulation of the skeletal and muscular systems. An osteopath may prescribe drugs, perform surgery and in some states are admitted to the staffs of general hospitals. In others, they must utilize osteopathic or proprietary hospitals.

FINDING THE PRIMARY CARE PHYSICIAN

This then is the choice for primary physicians: GP, FP, internist or osteopath. It's not easy to find a family physician in a strange place. At home, you can depend upon the experience your parents or relatives have had with their family physicians. Once you start out in a new area, it's not so easy.

One way is to ask your county medical society for a separate list of general practitioners, family practitioners and internists in your area. Your state osteopathic association can supply a list of osteopaths in your area. Neither of these groups will make recommendations. Some county societies have a "rotation" referral plan and won't even give you a full list, just the three or so names which have come "up to the top of the list."

The second method is to check hospitals in your area, particularly if you are in an urban or metropolitan area. You check with the administration office of each hospital and ask for a list of the GPs, FPs and internists "on the staff" of the hospital. You might also ask if osteopaths are admitted to the staff of that hospital.

There are three types of hospital: 1) public, run by a government agency, 2) non-profit or "community" hospital, supported by donations from the community, and 3) proprietary hospitals, run for profit by a group of doctors or a company specializing in hospital care. The ones with the toughest standards, both medical (good) and political or social (bad) for their staff positions, are usually the teaching hospitals.

After getting all these lists, where do you go next? Well, a doctor in a major urban area who practices on the staff of more than one hospital may be a good choice. But it's not always a good indication of the skill or ability of the physician, merely activity.

I have personally had good luck with local pharmacists, the ones behind the prescription counter of your local drugstore. I find the ones in privately owned pharmacies are usually more knowledgeable than those who man the prescription counters of chain drugstores — mainly because the independent pharmacist stays put longer and knows the physicians in the area better.

When the list is worked down to a few names, the local pharmacist might be asked to comment on the various physicians, from the standpoint of their age, personality, etc. If you know a nurse or other health professional, the same approach might be taken. Not every health professional knows every doctor, unless you are in a rather samll community, but there are a number that can be described.

FIND OUT COSTS

Once you get the leads to a manageable number of names, call the offices of each and ask what the fees are for: 1) an initial visit (which will cost more because a medical history must be taken and because the doctor must examine you thoroughly), and 2) regular visits. The receptionist who answers the phone (not an answering service) can tell you this.

You aren't liable to find any great bargains this way, but you will screen out any which have unusually high charges for the area. Once you've established this, you pick one out and make an initial appointment — for the whole family at once — telling the receptionist that you are looking for a "family" doctor. It won't get you a discount on the rate, but it will give the whole family an opportunity to get to know the doctor and for him or her to get to know the family.

EVALUATE THE DOCTOR

Don't just go in, sit there and then leave again. Evaluate the doctor. After all, you are looking for a supplier of primary care who will treat you and your family for a long time.

Does the doctor take a complete medical history? Does he take it, not the receptionist? In order to treat you properly, he must know everything that has happened to you medically.

Does the doctor ask specific questions about your present state of health and sense of well-being? Questions like: "How are you feeling now?" "Do you have anything bothering you?" "Do you smoke?" "Do you drink?" "How much?" "How is your sex life?" From the last question, it is obvious that, although you may all visit the doctor at the same time, he should take you one by one for determining such areas of personal health and outlook.

One area of initial evaluation is the doctor's waiting room. If it is clean, neat and comfortable, that's a plus. If it isn't, the doctor may not be much concerned with his or her patients as "people." The doctor's office is another clue. If it's neat and clean, the chances are that his or her care is equally precise. If it's messy and dirty, watch out.

If you have weight problems, a fat doctor is probably not the one for you. If you smoke too much, a doctor who smokes is probably not going to be convincing in telling you to give it up. On the other hand, a doctor who obviously keeps in condition and observes a healthy way of life is probably going to recommend the same thing for you and your family.

THE PEDIATRICIAN

If you have children, you are probably looking for a pediatrician, as well. If you have a family doctor, he can recommend a pediatrician. That's a good reason for finding your family physician for primary care first. On the other hand, if your children are past the infant stage — where the pediatrician is most desired — you may prefer to have your family doctor handle the children as well as the adults.

Your choice of a primary care physician is the key to this. An internist is primarily an adult health specialist, just as the pediatrician is a child health specialist. If you have an internist, you may well decide to have a pediatrician for your children up through or into adolescence. On the other hand, if you have a GP or FP, or an osteopath in general practice, you might want the whole family's health in a single pair of hands.

The pediatrician is one of the most overworked and underpaid of all the physicians today. Mothers, particularly with first borns, are never loath to rouse the pediatrician at an ungodly hour of the night. But infant care is a distinct specialty, and children under the age of three are the specialty of the pediatrician, who probably runs a well baby clinic, a camp innoculation service and a hectic practice of colds, flu, scrapes, bruises, intestinal upsets, etc. — all at the same time.

THE OB/GYN

Many women look to the gynecologust as their primary care physician, but that is probably a mistake. While the gynecologist is concerned with menstruation, fertility, the glandular system of the female — the speciality does not go much beyond the pelvic area. Thus, experience in other illness and disease is not as extensive as for the GP, FP, internist or osteopath.

An obstetrician, however, is recommended for care during pregnancy and delivery. Since most specialists embrace both obstetrics and gynecology, it is not uncommon for a woman to continue to see her OB/GYN specialist long after the baby has been born. However, it is desireable for her to see her family physician on a regular basis as well.

THE SPECIALIST

There is an entire shopping list of specialist physicians and surgeons available today, particularly in larger cities. To provide a brief description of what each is and does, the list below covers the majority of such specialties:

Allergist - This is a specialist who focusses upon the reactions arising from allergies. An allergist is not a distinct specialty; quite often it is an internist who has taken an interest in this field. Asthmatics may be treated by allergists, or may be taken care of by internists.

Cardiologists - These are heart doctors, and it is one of the most prestigious specialties —

with the highest rates — into which doctors can specialize.

Dermatologists - Derma means skin, so these are skin doctors. One hospital joke goes: "Dermatologists have three treatments. If it's wet, dry it. If it's dry, wet it. If it's red, use steroids."

Endocrinologists - The endocrinologist is a specialist in hormone (gland) diseases and abnormalities.

Gastroenterologists - these are specialists in the digestive system: stomach, bowels, liver, gall bladder, pancreas and esophagus.

Infectious Disease Specialists - These are internists who have selected the infectious disease as an area of specialty. They are found primarily in larger cities.

Nephrologists - These are specialists in kidney problems.

Neurologists - Specialists in the nervous system.

Obstreticians/Gynecologists - These are specialists in the female reproductive system. Obstreticians specialize in pregnancies and births.

Oncologists - Specialists in tumors and cancer.

Opthamologists - Specialists in the eyes.

Orthopedists - These are bone docotors.

Otolaryngologists - Specialists in problems and diseases of the ears, nose and throat.

Pediatricians - These are specialists in health of infants, children and even adolescents.

Psychiatrists - Physicians who specialize in mental health.

There are a number of physicians who specialize in surgery. The general surgeon, the most common outside the large cities, takes on all types of surgery, but even here, some cases require referral to specialists who have the skills and experience on specific areas of the body.

Cardiac Surgeons - Specialize in heart surgery.

Cardiovascular Surgeons - Specialists in surgery of the blood vessels associated with the heart.

Neuorsurgeons - Specialists in surgery of the nervous system.

Plastic Surgeons - Specialists in reconstructive surgery. Their greatest activity is in cosmetic surgery on the face and breasts.

Proctologists - Specialists in surgery of the bowels.

Thoracic Surgeons - Specialists in surgery of the chest.

Urologists - Specialists in the urinary tract, including the prostate gland in men. While urologists see non-surgical patients with urological problems, they function as surgeons, particularly in the area of kidney and bladder stones and prostate resectioning and removal.

Vascular Surgeons - These specialists concentrate upon surgery of the blood vessel system.

There are also a number of medical specialists who do not have practices, but who operate primarily in hospitals. If you have a serious illness or an operation, you may encounter some of these physicians and their bills.

Anesthesologist - A physician who provides anesthetic during operations and monitors patients' life signs.

Hematologist - This is a blood doctor. His concerns are the function and condition of a patient's blood.

Pathologist - A physician who examines tissue and bone to deterimne if malignancy exists. They also conduct post mortem examinations.

Physiatrist - A physician who specializes in rehabilitation after illness or injury. Administers physical therapy.

Radiologist - A physician who interprets X-rays. Sub-specialties include angiographers, who specialize in cardiac catheritization (injecting radiopaque dye into the heart), nuclear medicine specialists who use radioactive materials for examination and treatment, and ultrasound specialists who use ultrasonic scanning equipment to examine patients.

GROUP PRACTICE

Instead of settling for a family doctor who is in independent practice — still the most common choice — many families are choosing an organization of doctors who provide a range of specialties under one roof. The group practice is when several physicians get together and share office space and, more important, facilities and equipment. While groups vary, there is usually an internist who often serves as the diagnostician for the group.

The advantage of group practice is that most of the medical needs of a patient can be found in the one organization, and the patient can be routed from one member of the group to another. Another advantage is that by sharing the cost of expensive equipment and laboratory facilities, the group can provide modern support services at a reasonable cost and without shuttling patients off in various directions to other facilities, sometimes at quite a distance.

It is usual in a group for the patient to see the same physician as a primary care supplier upon each office visit. This permits the conventional physician/patient relationship to develop. Consultation is simplified, and the patient receives the benefit of the combined skills and experience of the group members.

HEALTH MAINTENANCE ORGANIZATIONS (HMOs)

Health Maintenance Organizations are providers of total health care. For a specified fee, usually monthly, the HMO provides outpatient services (doctor visits, laboratory tests, etc.) and hospitalization. Some, like the original Kaiser-Permanente organization, have all of the various elements of the health care spectrum under one ownership. Others are basically a group practice which subcontracts out laboratory and hospital services as the subscriber (patient) requires them.

The greatest number of HMOs are associated with group medical plans, such as employer plans or union-sponsored employee plans. Some do not permit subscriptions from the general public.

OTHER HEALTH PROFESSIONALS

There are a number of other health professionals who are not physicians. Some work closely with physicians; others are not recognized by the medical profession.

Chiropractors are not physicians, although they use the title "doctor." They are specialists in manipulating the spine, and the major concern of most patients who consult them is back and neck pains. While chiropractors take X-rays and may do urine analyses, they are prohibited by law from prescribing medicine or performing surgery of any kind.

Opticians are technicians who grind lenses to correct vision. They are not physicians, and must have a prescription before they can dispense corrective glasses or contact lenses.

Optometrists are trained in visual refraction (measuring vision and prescribing corrective lenses). Although in some states they may use drops in the eye for examinations, they are not physicians and can neither prescribe medicines nor perform surgery. In some hospitals and clinics they work within and under the supervision of the opthamology department. They have received training in recognizing eye ailments and diseases, and will refer a patient with a medical condition to an opthamologist.

Podiatrists are foot doctors. While they are not physicians, they are trained in the care, treatment and surgery of the feet. They are found, as health professionals, on the staffs of many hospitals today. They use the letters DPM (Doctor of Podiatric Medicine) after their names. They were once called chiropodists, but that name has been superseded by podiatrist.

Psychologists are not physicians. They earn a PhD (Doctor of Philosophy) degree in psychology and function as mental health therapists and conduct mental health testing. They are often found working with physicians (psychiatrists) and in hospitals, where they function as health professionals.

There is another area of non-physician health professionals which has been growing. This includes nurse practioners and physician's assistants — grouped together as paramedical specialists.

Nurse Practioners are registered nurses who have received specialized training in certain areas of medical care. The use of nurse midwives to handle delivery is increasing. Nurse anesthetists are used in many smaller hospitals and may administer anesthesia in larger ones under the direction of a physician (anesthesiologist).

Physician's Assistants are persons trained in identifying and treating common and uncomplicated ailments and conditions. They work for a physician and handle much of the screening of patients to relieve the physician of much routine detail.

HANDLING MEDICAL EMERGENCIES

One of the most terrifying experiences is to have a member of the family injured or suddenly stricken ill. What to do? The most important action which you can take is to get prompt medical advice or treatment.

There are several options which you have in a medical emergency. (Too often, such emergencies occur on weekends or in the evening when the family doctor is not in the office.)

Family Doctor. Your family doctor should be asked on the first visit what actions should be taken if there is an emergency. He or she may have emergency numbers to call.

Emergency Ward of a hospital will probably be one of the suggestions the doctor will make. If the hospital maintains an emergency ward, there will be emergency physician care available.

Ambulance Service, whether supplied by a hospital, a police or fire department or a volunteer group, usually has well-trained paramedics who can handle routine emergencies, and by contacting a hospital, can often provide physician-directed, on-site stabilizing treatment.

The telephone numbers for each of these services should be listed in front of this book, posted on the back of the medicine cabinet door in your bathroom, and fastened to the base of your telephone so they can be found quickly in case of an emergency.

THE FAMILY MEDICAL KIT

The family medical kit should be kept in a specific place, and after any use, the materials should be replaced for the next time. The minimum contents should be:

A roll of adhesive tape (½″ or ¾″ in width)
A roll of gauze bandage (2″ wide)
Gauze dressings (2″ x 2″ in individual sterile packages)
Gauze dressings (4″ x 4″ in individual sterile packages)
Band-Aids (assorted sizes)
Antiseptic solution (spray can) or ointment
Aspirin (both child and adult strengths) or Tylenol
Cough medicine (recommended by your doctor)
Syrup of Ipecac (to induce vomiting)
Tweezers (to remove splinters and insect stingers)
Petroleum jelly (scrapes and abrasions)
Kaopectate (or equivalent for diarrhea)

The purpose of a family medical kit is to take care of minor colds, scrapes, bruises, cuts and burns. Anything more extensive should be immediately handled by the hospital emergency ward or the family doctor or pediatrician.

SELECTING THE FAMILY DENTIST

The same problems in finding a suitable dentist for the family arise as in finding a family dcotor. However, if you find the doctor first, you have one major advantage: The doctor will usually be willing to refer you to a dentist whose work he knows.

The field of dentistry has also been fragmented by specialization. However, there are far more "general practice" dentists than there are M.D.s in general practice. The specialists which the family are most likely to come into contact with are:

Orthodontists are dentists who specialize in correction of teeth misalignment, poor bite, etc. Orthodontists are the most prevalent dental specialists, amounting to more than 6 percent of all dentists.

Pedontists are a growing field. These are dentists who specialize in children's dentistry. Some specialize both in dental work for children and orthodontics.

Periodontists are dentists who specialize in problems of the gums. As we all get older, we will be more likely to visit the periodontist, particularly if the task of regular dental hygiene hasn't been practiced diligently.

Exodontists are oral surgeons. Even though most dentists have a degree as a Doctor of Dental Surgery (D.D.S.), most complex surgery is performed by exodontists — who like to be called oral surgeons or maxillo-facial surgeons.

Prosthodontists are specialists in providing artificial substitutes for teeth: dentures, bridges, tooth implants, etc.

Endodontists are specialists in root canal work. You'll find them primarily in or near large cities, for there are relatively few of these specialists, yet the field is growing because the increasing interest of patients in keeping their teeth instead of having an abscessed tooth extracted.

Your family dentist may have either a D.D.S. degree or a Doctor of Dental Medicine (D.D.M.). Both degrees are approximately the same, but given by different dental colleges. Your family dentist, like the family doctor who is a general practitioner, has had some training in each of the specialty areas listed above.

He will probably be able to do simple orthodontics if your child's teeth are not too badly out of line, will be able to do root canal work, gum treatment and surgery, tooth extraction, make dentures (or at least take the impressions for a dental mechanic to make), and take care of your children's teeth.

However, most family dentists will refer the very complex cases to a specialist, particularly oral surgery and gum disease. The only specialist you may consult directly, without going through your family dentist, is the pedontist — the children's dentist. In this case, it's much like the pediatrician; recommendations are usually passed from mother to mother, based on how well her children are taken care of by that specialist. Pedontists often stress the application of fluorides to children's teeth during the growing years.

SAVE YOUR TEETH

It is far less common today to find the kind of dentist (except in dental "mills") who says, "Better have all your teeth out. That way you won't run into any more problems." The stress today is upon saving the natural teeth.

This starts with childhood and care for the "baby" teeth, which, although they will fall out, must be taken care of to insure that the adult teeth come in properly and without disease. It continues through childhood, where the good habits of cleaning and brushing are formed, and into adulthood, where regular cleanings and tooth care insure freedom from gum disease and decay.

Reduction of sugar in the diet, regular brushing, frequent visits to the dentist, and an adequate diet, particularly of all of the vitamins and minerals, keep children's teeth and gums healthy and insure good dental habits as an adult.

The greatest cause of teeth loss in adults is gum disease. This is primarily caused by allowing plaque to build up at the base of teeth. If allowed to build up, plaque turns into the harder calculus (tartar), which cuts into the gums and causes gum disease. By having teeth cleaned regularly, by the dentist or a dental technician in the dentist's office, this plaque is removed and the danger of irritation to the gums is reduced. Everyone's buildup of plaque and calculus is at a different rate; your dentist can tell you how often you should have your teeth cleaned. With some individuals it is once a year, with others it is once every three months.

Because of the rapidity of cavity development in softer children's and adolescents' teeth, you should make sure they are examined by a dentist at least once each six months. Be sure that the dentist is liked by the children. Too often, rough or scary treatment in childhood is responsible for adults never visiting a dentist, "because it *hurts!*"

QUICK DICTIONARY
of
CONDITIONS, TESTS and TREATMENTS

A

ABDOMINAL CRAMP See *INTESTINAL CRAMP, CRAMP.*

ABORTION Emptying the uterus of a fetus prior to the fourth month of pregnancy. Terminating a pregnancy.

ABSCESS A localized area of infection marked by a collection of pus.

ACARIASIS An infestation of mites. See *MITE.*

ACCUPRESSURE A method of pain relief using fingertip pressure on the same points as used in accupuncture.

ACCUPUNCTURE Treatment of ailments by inserting needles through the skin in pre-determined points, often remote from site of actual disorder or pain.

ACHLORHYDRIA Failure of the stomach to produce hydrochloric acid to digest food.

ACHONDROPLASIA A congenital bone condition resulting in dwarfism. See *DWARFISM.*

ACIDOSIS A reduction of the normal alkaline balance of the body.

ACID PHOSPHATASE TEST A key test for cancer of the prostate. Acid phosphatase is an enzyme produced by the male prostate. Cancer, prostate infection and some blood diseases, as well as rectal prostate massage, will increase blood levels of acid phosphatase.

ACNE A skin condition in which oily secretions from overactive sebaceous (grease) glands and often dirt collect in the pores, causing infection and pimples. Extreme forms (acne vulgaris) leave pits and scars. Most common in adolescense.

ACNE ROSACEA Flushing of the face, generally the nose and cheeks. Initially from hot drinks, meals, changing from cold to hot areas, etc. Becomes permanent. Also *CAULIFLOWER NOSE, POTATO NOSE.*

ACRODYNIA See *ERYTHREDEMA POLYNEUROPATHY.*

ACROMEGALY Giantism resulting from overproduction of the pituitary gland after maturity. Includes heavy jaw, overhanging bulging forehead, excessive size of hands, etc. See *GIGANTISM.*

ACROPHOBIA Fear of high places, heights.

ACTINOMYCOSIS A fungus infection contracted from animals.

ADDICTION True addition (opposed to habit) is when there exists: 1. uncontrollable craving for a substance, 2. increasing tolerance to it, and 3. physical dependence upon it.

ADDISONIAN ANEMIA See *PERNICIOUS ANEMIA.*

ADDISON'S DISEASE An adrenal gland disorder which causes muscular weakness and a bronze tone to the skin.

ADENOIDS Enlarged lymph glands at the back of the area where the nose and throat join (the nasopharynx). Extreme enlargement blocks breathing and gives a "nasal" tone to speaking.

ADENOMA Cancer of the glands.

ADHESION Abnormal union of two surfaces as a result of inflammation or surgery.

ADIPOSIS See *OBESITY.*

ADJUSTMENT Manipulation of joints.

AEROPHOBIA 1. fear of flying, and 2. fear of drafts.

AGUE Violent shivering at the beginning of a fever, such as malaria.

AIR SICKNESS See *MOTION SICKNESS.*

ALBINO Congenital lack of pigment in skin, hair and iris of the eye.

ALBUMIN TEST A blood test for liver function (albumin is produced in the liver), for kidney disease and malnutrition. Low blood albumin permits edema (collection of fluid in the tissues). Normal range is 3.5 to 5.5 grams per 100 milliliters (g/100 ml).

ALBUMINURIA Presence of albumin in the urine, usually as a result of kidney disease.

ALCOHOLISM An illness marked by the excessive use of alcohol. See *ADDICTION.*

ALEXIA Inability to read. May be caused by a number of conditions.

ALKALINE PHOSPHATASE TEST A test for liver and bone disease. High levels of this enzyme in the blood, combined with high bilirubin (jaundice) may also signal gallstone blockage of bile ducts or tumors of the bile system. High levels of alkaline phosphatase alone may indicate over dosage of vitamin D, use of common medications (oral contraceptives, sedatives, hormones, oral antidiabetics, antibiotics, blood pressure reducers or gout medicines). May also indicate tumor of the parathyroid gland.

ALKALOSIS An increase in the normal alkaline balance of the body.

ALLERGEN A substance which produces allergy symptoms. Also *ANTIGEN.*

ALLERGIC RHINITIS See *HAY FEVER.*

ALLERGY A reaction caused by sensitivity to certain substances or conditions. May include rashes, swellings, inflamed eyes, rhinitis.

ALOPECIA See *BALDNESS*.

ALOPECIA AREATA A form of baldness caused by emotional stress or tensions. The hair falls out in patches, leaving a "motheaten" appearance. With or without treatment, the hair will grow back in several months to several years.

AMAUROSIS Blindness from disease of the retina or optic nerve.

AMBLYOPIA Poor sight in a healthy eye, which cannot be fully corrected. Most commonly caused by suppression or lack of use. See *EXANOPSIA*.

AMEBIASIS A bacterial infection of the bowels.

AMENORRHEA Stopping or lack of menstruation not connected with pregnancy.

AMNESIA Sudden and complete loss of memory.

AMNIOCENTESIS A test of fluid from around the live fetus, taken by inserting a needle into the uterus. Used to check for genetically related diseases and fetal development.

AMOEBIC DYSENTERY Dysentery caused by intestinal infestation by amoeba. See *DYSENTERY*.

AMYOTROPHIC LATERAL SCLEROSIS A deterioration of the spinal cord resulting in muscular atrophy.

ANAL FISSURE A cleft, furrow or slit in the anal tissue at the junction of the skin and mucous membrane. Suspected cause is straining because of constipation.

ANAL FISTULA A penetrating ulcer creating a tunnel from the rectum to the skin. Stays open because of contamination and irritation by feces.

ANALGESIC A substance which reduces pain.

ANAPHYLACTIC SHOCK See *ANAPHYLAXIS*.

ANAPHYLACTOID See *ANAPHYLAXIS*.

ANAPHYLAXIS Severe allergic reaction, sometimes fatal. Caused by various substances, such as penicillin and other drugs, bee stings. Also *ANAPHYLACTIC SHOCK*.

ANCYLOSTOMIASIS Also *ANCYLOSTOMA*. See *HOOKWORMS*.

ANEMIA A deficiency in red blood corpuscles or in hemoglobin content of the red corpuscles. See *IRON DEFICIENCY ANEMIA, PERNICIOUS ANEMIA*.

ANESTHESIA A numbing or loss of pain from the injection, ingestion or inhalation of a drug.

ANEURYSM A swollen or distended area in a blood vessel wall.

ANGINA A closing or choking. Usually short form for angina pectoris. See *ANGINA PECTORIS*.

ANGINA PECTORIS Heart pain caused by insufficiency of blood supply to the heart muscle as a result of narrowing or choking off of the arteries supplying the heart. See *ARTERIOSCLEROSIS, CORONARY ARTERY DISEASE, INFARCTION*.

ANGIODEMA A severe form of hives which may also affect the joints.

ANGIOGRAM Special X-ray studies in which a radiopaque dye is injected into the bloodstream to detect narrowing of heart blood vessels. See *CARDIAC CATHETERIZATION*.

ANGIOMA A tumor composed of blood vessels, usually harmless. Also *BIRTHMARK, NEVUS*.

ANISEIKONA Images seen by each eye are different in size or shape.

ANKYLOSING SPONDYLITIS Rheumatic inflammation of the spine, reducing mobility of the vertebrae. Related to rheumatoid arthritis. See *SPONDYLITIS*.

ANKYLOSIS Loss of movement in a joint, generally from severe arthritis or injury. Also may be surgically induced to alleviate pain.

ANOREXIA Loss of appetite.

ANOREXIA NERVOSA Neurotic condition where young women control eating to less than necessary to live, while convincing themselves they are benefiting themselves.

ANOXEMIA See *ANOXIA*.

ANOXIA Shortage of oxygen in the blood. Also *ANOXEMIA*.

ANTACID A substance to overcome excess stomach acid or to turn urine alkaline.

ANTHRAX Bacterial infection carried by cattle and sheep. Symptoms are boils and lung infection. Also *WOOL SORTER'S DISEASE*.

ANTIBIOTIC Medicine which checks the growth of bacteria. Not effective against viruses.

ANTIBIOTIC SENSITIVITY TEST A laboratory test of a sample of bacterial infection by exposing it to various antibiotics to determine effectiveness of the drugs.

ANTIBODY A substance produced by the body to fortify itself against disease organisms.

ANTICOAGULANT A substance which is used to prevent blood clots.

ANTIGEN A protein which produces allergic reactions. Also *ALLERGEN*.

ANTIHISTAMINE A medicine which neutralizes histamine (a natural substance produced by the body in reaction to allergic materials).

ANTIMETROPIA One eye is nearsighted, the other farsighted.

ANTIPERSPIRANT A preparation which reduces perspiration, particularly under arms. See *DEODORANT*.

ANTIPRURITIC A medicine to alleviate itching.

ANTISEPTIC A substance which kills bacteria and bacterial infection upon direct contact.

ANTITOXIN A substance created by the body to fight poisons from bacteria (toxins) and which may be injected into others to prevent a disease.

ANTITUSSIVE A substance used to reduce mucus.

ANXIETY 1. A state of fear. See *PHOBIA*. 2. A neurotic reaction. See *HYSTERIA*.

AORTOCORONARY BYPASS SURGERY An operation to relieve coronary artery blockage. A section of blood vessel is grafted into the coronary artery to by-pass the blockage. See *CORONARY ARTERY DISEASE.*

AORTOGRAPHY An X-ray examination of the major artery in the body. A catheter is inserted into the groin and a radiopaque substance is injected into the aorta.

APHASIA Inability to communicate with words.

APHONIA Loss of the ability to speak.

APOPLEXY A sudden loss of consciousness, followed by paralysis due to cerebral hemorrhage or blockage of the artery of the brain by an embolus or thrombosis. See *EMBOLUS, THROMBOSIS, STROKE.*

APPENDICITIS Inflammation of the appendix, usually accompanied by raised white blood cell (leucocyte) count, fever and abdominal pain.

APPETITE LOSS A loss of appetite can be a clue to various conditions. Important as a diagnostic tool. See *ANOREXIA.*

APHTHOUS STOMATITIS Ulcer of the mouth. Also *CANKER SORE.*

ARACHNODACTYLY Hereditary condition involving fingers and toes much longer and thinner than normal. See *SPIDER FINGERS.*

ARCUS SENILIS A white circle or arc at the edge of the cornea. Common in aging eyes but harmless.

ARRHYTHMIA Any disturbance of the natural rhythm of the heart. Also *TACHYCARDIA* and *FIBRILLATION.*

ARTERIOSCLEROSIS Loss of elasticity of the arteries, causing inability to expand to increase circulation in response to exertion. Also *HARDENING OF THE ARTERIES.*

ARTHRITIS Inflammation of a joint. See *GOUT, OSTEOARTHRITIS, RHEUMATOID ARTHRITIS.*

ARTHROCENTESIS A test to determine the cause of joint inflammation. A needle is inserted into the joint for a sample of joint fluid.

ARTHROGRAPHY An X-ray study of a joint. Air, gas or a radiopaque substance is injected into the joint.

ARTHROPLASTY An operation to reconstruct or replace a joint.

ARTHROSCOPY An examination of the inside of a joint by inserting an arthroscope tube through a surgical incision.

ARTIFICIAL RESPIRATION Various methods to keep a person breathing when normal automatic function has stopped. See *CPR.*

ASBESTOSIS Inflammation or irritation of the lungs from asbestos dust.

ASCITES Edema of the abdomen. See *DROPSY, EDEMA.*

ASPHYXIA Unconsciousness due to lack of oxygen.

ASPIRATION Removal of liquid by suction.

ASPIRATION TEST A test of the digestive tract by removing digestive secretions through a tube inserted down the subject's throat.

ASTHENIA Loss of strength. Also *FEEBLENESS.*

ASTHENOPIA Eye strain.

ASTHMA A condition involving recurrent attacks of shortness of breath, wheezing, coughing due to spasmodic contraction of the bronchial tubes.

ASTIGMATISM An eye abnormality which prevents a line from being seen in focus evenly along its length.

ATAXIA Loss of muscular coordination.

ATELECTASIS A lung condition in which small air chambers collapse.

ATHEROSCLEROSIS See *ARTERIOSCLEROSIS.*

ATHLETE'S FOOT A fungus infection, generally between the toes. It is highly contagious, transmitted in showers, damp floors or by direct contact. May also occur in the groin. Related to ringworm.

ATOPIC DERMATITIS A skin irritation caused by contact with such things as soap, detergent, wool, dyes, cosmetics. See *ECZEMA.*

ATOPY An allergy where there is a family history of allergy and an immediate allergic response to a skin test. Also *CLINICAL ALLERGY.*

ATRESIA Blockage of a passage, such as the ear canal.

ATROPHY A wasting or withering of a part of the body. Shrinking of a muscle.

AUDIOMETRY A hearing test using an electrical instrument: the audiometer.

AUSCULATION Examination by listening to sounds of the chest or other parts of the body by an instrument (stethoscope) which transmits sound to the doctor's ears.

AUTOIMMUNE DISEASE A disease caused by allergic reaction to the subject's own body tissues.

AUTOPSY An examination of the body and contents after death. Also *POST MORTEM.*

B

B.C.D. A tuberculosis vacine.

BMR (BASAL METABOLIC RATE) A test to determine the rate at which the body consumes fuel (food).

BUN (BLOOD UREA NITROGEN) TEST A key test of kidney function. Urea is the end product of protein metabolism by the cells and is removed from the blood by the kidneys. High blood urea arises generally from kidney failure, but also from burns, intestinal hemorrhage and tumors. The test may also be affected by some antibiotics, diuretics, sedatives and bloodpressure reducing drugs. Normal range is 10 to 25 milligrams per 100 milliliters (mg/100 ml).

BABINSKY TEST A test of spinal cord condition by scraping the sole of the foot.

BACKACHE A pain in the back, arising from any of a number of causes, both mechanical (ruptured discs) and muscular. Also *LUMBAGO.*

BAGASSOSIS Deposits of bagasse (sugar cane stalk) dust in the lung.

BALDNESS Loss of hair. Most common form is "male pattern baldness" where the crown of the head becomes bare, leaving hair around the sides and back.

See *ALOPECIA, ALOPECIA AREATA.*

BALLISTOCARDIOGRAPHY Measurement of the strength of the heart by placing the subject on a special table which records blood pulsing.

BALLOON TECHNIQUE Use of balloons which are inflated at the site of a problem to: 1. open blood vessels which are clogged with deposits, 2. apply medication.

BANG'S DISEASE See *BRUCELLOSIS.*

BARANY BOX A hearing test utilizing a funnel-shaped instrument (the Barany box).

BARBER'S ITCH Bacterial infection around the roots of the beard. Also *SYCOSIS BARBAE.*

BARBITURATE A sedative (hypnotic) drug. Addictive.

BARIUM ENEMA Radiopaque barium is introduced into the lower bowel (colon) and rectum by an enema to permit X-ray examination. Also *LOWER GI SERIES.*

BASAL METABOLISM The process of using food to fuel the body. The conversion of food to energy and waste. See *BMR.*

BED SORE Sore caused by constant pressure which prevents blood circulation. Most commonly occurring where bones are close to the surface: buttocks, hips, ankles, heels. Can be prevented by good nursing, frequent position changes, cushioning and skin hygiene. Also *DECUBITUS.*

BED WETTING Although most children stop voiding urine during sleep by the end of the third year, some continue. Cause may be inflammation of the urinary system, but is generally unknown. Also *ENURESIS.*

BEE STING Bee, hornet and wasp stings inject venom which causes temporary pain and welts, but are usually harmless. In some individuals who are allergic, however, it may cause severe reactions. See *ANAPHYLACTIC SHOCK.*

BEKESY TEST A hearing test to localize the area of nerve damage.

BELCH Expulsion of gas or air from the stomach through the esophagus and mouth.

BELL'S PALSY Paralysis of the facial nerve, causing a relaxation of the facial muscles on the side of the face. The result is a lopsided look.

BENIGN Any self-limiting condition which is not life threatening.

BERI BERI Nerve inflammation, often accompanied by edema in the legs. Caused by deficiency of vitamin B_1 (thiamine hydrochloride).

BILIOUSNESS Any digestive disturbance. See *DYSPEPSIA, NAUSEA.*

BILIRUBIN TEST Key test of liver function. Bilirubin is a yellow pigment created from breakdown of red blood cells and excreted (as bile) through the liver. High levels in the blood cause jaundice. Normal range in blood is less than 1.2 milligrams per 100 milliliters (mg/100 ml). See *JAUNDICE.*

BIFOCAL A spectacle or contact lens with two focusing distances, one for near, one for far.

BIOMICROSCOPE An instrument for examining the eye under magnification. See *SLITLAMP.*

BIOPSY The microscopic examination of a portion of the body by taking a sample.

BIORHYTHMS Short for biological rhythms, which are body activity levels which change by season, time of month and time of day.

BIRTH CONTROL See *CONTRACEPTION.*

BIRTHMARK A congenital skin blemish. There are different types: pigmented nevus (mole); vascular nevus, which include the strawberry mark and the port wine stain.

BLACK DEATH See *BUBONIC PLAGUE.*

BLACK EYE Bruise of the area around the eye. See *BRUISE.*

BLACKHEAD A plug of partially dried greasy material in a pore, the opening of a sebaceous (grease) gland. Also *COMEDO.*

BLACKOUT Sudden loss of consciousness, usually temporary.

BLASTOMYCOSIS A fungus infection causing tumors of the skin. May also affect internal organs and bones. See *ACTINOMYCOSIS.*

BLEB A blister on skin or cornea, filled with fluid or blood. See *BLISTER.*

BLEPHAREDEMA Swelling of the eyelids.

BLEPHARITIS Inflammation of the eyelids.

BLEPHAROSPASM Twitching of the eyelids. Often caused by eye strain.

BLISTER A pocket of fluid formed beneath the top layer of skin.

BLOOD BLISTER A pocket of blood formed beneath the top layer of skin.

BLOOD CLOT Clotting is a chemical change in one of the plasma proteins (fibrinogen), which forms the blood into a firm mass which may be large enough to block a blood vessel. See *THROMBOSIS.*

BLOOD GAS TEST A blood test to determine the levels of oxygen and carbon dioxide.

BLOOD LIPID (FAT) LEVELS Cholesterol levels and other blood fats, such as triglicerides, are determined by taking a sample of blood. Average cholesterol level for American adults is 250 milligrams per 100 milliliters (mg/100 ml).

BLOOD POISONING An infection, first of the lymph system, then of the blood. Often arising from untreated infection of a finger or toe which spreads along the limb, associated with red streaks indicating speed of the spreading. See *LYMPHANGITIS, SEPTICEMIA, TOXEMIA.*

BLUE BABY A newborn baby with the telltale blue complexion of partial asphyxia. Indicates a congenital heart defect or blood deficiency which deprives the cells of oxygen.

BODY ODOR See *BROMIDROSIS.*

BOIL Small abscess resulting from an infected pore or hair follicle. Painful for several days but usually bursts and heals itself. Also *FURNUCLE*.

BOOSTERS Injections of immunizing materials to reinforce effects of earlier immunizations.

BONE MARROW TEST A test in which a needle is inserted into a bone, usually the hipbone or breastbone, and a sample of marrow removed.

BORBORYGMUS Rumbling of gas in the abdomen.

BORNHOLM'S DISEASE See *PLEURODYNIA*.

BOTULISM An often deadly form of food poisoning caused by an organism found in the ground. Improper canning encourages growth which generates a gas. A swelled can is often an indication of botulism and should always be discarded and destroyed. See *FOOD POISONING*.

BOWLEGS A condition where the knees do not touch when standing erect with ankles together. Natural in infants, but extreme cases may require splints until bones harden.

BRAIN SCAN A test for brain abnormalities (abscess, tumor) involving a radioactive substance injected into a neck artery and use of a scanning camera.

BRAIN FEVER See *ENCEPHALITIS*.

BREAST LUMPS Hard tissue areas in the fatty breast tissue. May be cysts or tumors (benign or malignant). Should be immediately reported to a doctor.

BREATH HOLDING Children often learn to hold their breath to gain attention or get what they want, sometimes to the point of momentary loss of consciousness. However, the automatic breathing reflex then takes over and no harm results. See *TANTRUM*.

BREECH BIRTH Instead of the normal head first birth, in breech birth the baby is born feet or buttocks first. This may involve turning the baby in the womb so the head emerges first.

BRIGHT'S DISEASE A kidney infection leading to edema, inability to properly extract water from the system, and high blood pressure. See *NEPHRITIS*.

BROMIDROSIS Strong body odor from action of harmless skin bacteria upon perspiration.

BRONCHIAL ASTHMA A chronic asthmatic condition involving the bronchial tubes. See *ASTHMA*.

BRONCHIECTASIS A complication of lung infection or bronchial asthma in which sections of the bronchial tubes become dilated to form pouches which fill with mucus and pus.

BRONCHITIS Inflammation of the bronchi (bronchial tubes) which carry oxygen from the trachea into the lungs and carbon dioxide back to the trachea.

BRONCHOEDEMA A condition in which the lining of the bronchial tubes swell and hinder airflow, usually associated with bronchial asthma.

BRONCHOGRAPHY An X-ray examination of the respiratory system after a radiopaque substance has been injected through a catheter into the bronchi.

BRONCHOSCOPY Inspection of the airway with an instrument (bronchoscope) which provides both light and a view of the trachea, bronchi and upper lung.

BRONCHOSPIROMETRY A breathing test involving blocking of a lung while measuring output of the other.

BRUCELLOSIS A cattle disease due to bacteria. Humans generally contact it handling infected cattle or drinking unpasteurized milk. Also *BANG'S DISEASE, MALTA FEVER*. See *UNDULANT FEVER*.

BRUISE Bleeding into the skin from a blow or pressure which ruptures veins below the skin. Losing oxygen, the blood turns blue, then green and yellow as it decomposes and is absorbed. Also *CONTUSION, ECCHYMOSIS, PURPURA*.

BUBONIC PLAGUE A severe infectious fever with swollen, acutely inflamed lymph nodes (called buboes) in groin, armpits and sides of the neck. Bleeding into the skin causes dark blotches, giving the disease the name "black death."

BUERGER'S DISEASE A disease of heavy smokers where small veins and arteries narrow, restricting blood circulation, especially to the extremeties. Also *THROMBOANGILITIS OBLITERANS*.

BUNION A deformity of the big toe from wearing improperly fitting shoes. The base "knuckle" protrudes and its bursa becomes inflamed and tender. Severe conditions require correction by surgery.

BURN Damage of skin and flesh by heat. First degree burns cause the skin to turn red. Second degree burns cause redness and blisters; 50% to 60% of body skin area so burned can be fatal. Third degree burns destroy skin layers, causing shock and later scarring.

BURSITIS Inflammation of the bursa, a closed sac containing fluid, located in joints or where a tendon slides over a bone.

C

CAT (COMPUTERIZED AXIAL TOMOGRAPHY) SCAN An examination of the body or head by a computer-driven X-ray machine which produces views of the subject which simulate "slices" taken through the body.

CBC (COMPLETE BLOOD COUNT) A blood test in which microscopic counts are made of both red and white blood cells. See *RBC* and *WBC*.

CCU (CORONARY CARE UNIT) A special hospital section for intensive heart care.

CDH (CONGENITAL DISLOCATION OF THE HIP) Usually caused by lax ligaments permitting the joint to slip in and out of place. If detected shortly after birth, it may be cured by splinting or putting the child in a cast.

CNT (CARDIOVASCULAR NUCLEAR TESTING) A radiation test for heart disease. A radioactive substance is injected into a vein and a camera scans its progress through the heart.

CPR (CARDIOPULMONARY RESUSCITATION) A combination of chest massage to compress and relax the heart and continue blood circulation and mouth-to-mouth artificial respiration to provide a supply of oxygen to the blood.

CACHEXIA Wasting and weakness caused by illness.

CAESAREAN SECTION Delivery of a baby by making an incision through the abdominal wall and the uterus wall.

CALCULUS 1. Chalky deposit on teeth, precipitated from saliva. Also *TARTAR*. 2. A "stone" in any hollow organ, such as kidneys, bladder, gall bladder and bile ducts. Composed mainly of calcium salts. See *GALL STONES, KIDNEY STONES*.

CALLOUS 1. Hard, thick outer layer of skin formed at the site of continued friction or pressure. 2. Hard tissue formed at the site of a bone break which later turns into new bone.

CAMP ITCH See *SCABIES*.

CANCER A malignant tumor or growth. Also *NEOPLASM, MALIGNANCY*.

CANDIDA A vaginal yeast infection with a discharge.

CANITIES Grey hair.

CANKER SORE See *APHTHOUS STOMATITIS*.

CAPUT SUCCEDANEUM An edemic swelling of the scalp of a newborn baby caused by pressure. It disappears within a few days without harm.

CARBOHYDRATE INTOLERANCE Lack of enzyme in intestines, leading to inability to convert sugars into forms available for digestion. Causes discomfort, flatulence and diarrhea. See *MALABSORPTION*.

CARBUNCLE Bacterial infection similar to a boil only larger and deeper. Usually found on the back of the neck, more common in adult males.

CARCINOMA Malignant growth in the skin and covering and lining tissues throughout the body. See *CANCER*.

CARDIAC CATHETERIZATION An examination of the heart by inserting a catheter (tube) into a blood vessel and threading it into the heart where pressure and oxygen can be measured and radiopaque material can be injected for X-ray pictures.

CARDIOGRAM See *EKG*.

CARIES Tooth decay. Also *CAVITY*.

CAROTID ARTERY TEST Test to detect restriction of bloodflow through arteries of the neck. See *DIRECTIONAL DOPPLER ULTRASONOGRAPHY, CAROTID PHONOANGIOGRAPHY, OCULOPLETHYSMOGRAPHY*.

CAROTID PHONOANGIOGRAPHY A test to measure bloodflow through the arteries of the neck.

CARRIER Individual harboring an infectious bacterium without having disease symptoms, but can infect others. Typhoid and diptheria may be "carried," often for years, in this manner.

CAR SICKNESS See *MOTION SICKNESS*.

CATALEPSY Self-induced or hysterical trance with the individual fixed in posture, often in unlikely positions.

CATARACT An opacity of the lens in the eye preventing clear vision. Most common in older people.

CATARRH Inflammation of mucous membranes of the nose. See *RHINITIS*.

CATARRH OF THE EAR See *SECRETORY OTITIS*.

CATATONIA Kind of trance where subject is still and rigid. Usually associated with severe schizophrenia. See *SCHIZOPHRENIA*.

CATHETER A flexible tube used to drain an organ (such as the urinary bladder), or to introduce substances into internal areas of the body.

CAT SCRATCH FEVER Viral infection transmitted by cat scratches. Abscess forms, lymph nodes swell in neck, armpits and groin, and there is frequently fever.

CAUDAL ANESTHESIA Anesthetic injected into the spine to deaden sensation below the waist. Used frequently in childbirth. Also *SADDLE BLOCK*.

CAULIFLOWER EAR Lumpy, deformed ear caused by scarring from repeated injury. Seen primarily in boxers.

CAUTERIZE The process of burning or searing a wound to control bleeding.

CAVITY See *CARIES*.

CEREBRAL ANGIOGRAPHY An X-ray test to determine blood clots, tumors, abscesses, irregularities in blood vessels, hemorrhages in the brain. Radioactive material is injected into the bloodstream.

CELIAC DISEASE An allergic condition in which certain foods produce in small children distended abdomens, and frothy, stinking diarrhea.

CELLULITIS Inflammation of tissue underlying the skin.

CEREBRAL PALSY Lack of control of voluntary movement with uncontrollable spasm of affected muscles. Due to failure of nerve cells in the brain. Also *SPASTIC PARALYSIS, LITTLE'S DISEASE*.

CEREBROSPINAL FEVER See *MENINGITIS*.

CERUMEN Ear wax.

CERVICITIS Inflammation of the cervix.

CHAFING Irritation of the skin from friction and dampness. Also *ERYTHEMA INTERTRIGO*.

CHALAZION Small round cysts on the eyelids.

CHANCRE Localized inflammation at the point of entry of an infection. The earliest sign of syphilis, a small, painless sore or lump of short duration. Sleeping sickness is also heralded by a chancre. See *SYPHILIS, SLEEPING SICKNESS*.

CHANCROID A venereal disease with a painful and persistent ulcer, often with swollen lymph nodes in the groin.

CHANGE OF LIFE See *MENOPAUSE*.

CHEMOTHERAPY Treatment of infection or malignancy with drugs which destroy bacteria or offending cells without seriously harming the patient.

CHICKEN POX A common infectious viral disease seen primarily in children since contracting the disease confers permanent immunity. A two-week incubation period is followed by fever, then a rash over several days, first on the body — usually the chest or abdomen

— then on face, arms and legs. Infectious until the last scab falls off. Scarring is rare. Also *VARICELLA*.

CHIGGERS (RED BUGS) Small insects which burrow into the skin and cause severe itching.

CHILBLAIN Blue-red raised welts on legs and arms caused by prolonged exposure to the cold.

CHILDBED FEVER See *PEURPERAL FEVER*.

CHILL Shivering attack due to illness, usually accompanied by fever. Also *RIGOR*.

CHLOASMA Splotches of pigment in the skin. Also *LIVER SPOTS*.

CHLOROSIS A secondary anemia which produces a pallor with a greenish tinge. Also *GREEN SICKNESS*.

CHOLANGIOGRAM See *INTRAVENOUS CHOLANGIOGRAM*.

CHOLECYSTITIS Cystitis of the gall bladder. See *CYSTITIS*.

CHOLECYSTOGRAPHY See *ORAL CHOLECYSTOGRAPHY*.

CHOLELITHIASIS Inflammation of the gall bladder.

CHOKING Spasmodic attempts to breathe caused by obstruction of the respiratory passages by strangulation, foreign objects, swelling.

CHOLERA A bacterial disease contracted from food or drinking water contaminated by feces from an infected person. Disease causes violent diarrhea with loss of body fluids, alkali and potassium salts, often fatal unless losses are replaced continuously during the course of the disease.

CHOREA MAJOR See *HUNTINGDON'S CHOREA*.

CHOREA MINOR Also *SYDENHAM'S CHOREA*. See *St. VITUS DANCE*.

CHORIOCARCINOMA A type of cancer affecting women who have been pregnant. It is rare.

CHRONIC A prolonged or recurrent condition.

CHRYSOTHERAPY Treatment of rheumatoid arthritis by injections of gold. Also *GOLD TREATMENT*.

CIRCUMCISION An operation to remove the foreskin from the penis.

CIRRHOSIS A liver disorder where damaged tissue has been replaced by scar tissue. May be associated with alcoholism and/or prolonged malnutrition. Frequently of no known origin.

CLAP See *GONORRHEA*.

CLAUDICATION A cramp-like pain in the legs during mild exercise. Caused by impaired circulation, usually due to fatty deposits in the arteries.

CLEFT PALATE A congenital defect of the roof of the mouth which opens into the nasal passages.

CLIMACTERIC See *MENOPAUSE*.

CLUB FOOT Deformity of the foot upon birth. Also *TALIPES*.

COCCIDIOSIS A parasitic infection of the lungs. Also *SAN JOAQUIN VALLEY FEVER*.

COELIAC DISEASE An early childhood disorder involving failure to assimilate certain foods, particularly fats. Diarrhea and malnutrition may result. May be caused by wheat and oats.

COLD See *COMMON COLD*.

COLD SORE Also *FEVER BLISTER*. See *HERPES SIMPLEX I*.

COLIC Intermittant pain, often severe from internal organs, caused by inflammation, obstruction or gas. Particularly seen in infants.

COLITIS Inflammation of the colon, commonly caused by bacterial food poisoning or dysentary.

COLLE'S FRACTURE A fracture of the forearm, usually from a fall on the palm of the hand.

COLONIC IRRIGATION A "high"enema. See *ENEMA*.

COLONOSCOPY An examination of the rectum and large bowel by a tubelike instrument inserted through the anus (colonoscope), which provides both light and a view of the colon.

COLOR BLINDNESS Inability to distinguish between certain colors, particularly red and green. A genetic defect, affecting more men than women.

COMA A state of unconsciousness from which the patient cannot be awakened.

COMEDO Also *COMEDONE*. See *BLACKHEADS*.

COMMON COLD Acute inflammation of mucous membranes of nose and throat due to a viral infection. Also *NASOPHARYNGITIS, CORYZA*.

COMPOUND FRACTURE A broken bone where the ends or splinters protrude through muscle and skin to open air.

COMPULSION An irresistible urge to do something repeatedly, such as washing hands or turning out lights. See *NEUROSIS*.

CONCUSSION A bruising of the brain from a blow to the head. Often accompanied by temporary loss of consciousness. There may be temporary amnesia (loss of memory) affecting periods immediately before the concussion.

CONFUSION Severe mental disorientation, often as a result of serious illness or senility.

CONGENITAL Existing from or before birth. Not necessarily hereditary.

CONJUNCTIVAL TEST A test for allergy in which a suspected substance is placed in the eye.

CONJUNCTIVITIS Inflammation of the covering (conjunctiva) of the white part of the eye. Highly contagious, spread by touching eye and then other items where other people can pick it up. Also *OPTHALMIA*.

CONSTIPATION Infrequent or difficult elimination of feces from the bowels, accompanied with hard stools.

CONSUMPTION A lung disease, particularly tuberculosis, which results in the patient wasting away (losing weight). See *TUBERCULOSIS, PHTHISIS*.

CONTACT DERMATITIS A class of skin problems resulting from irritation caused by coming into contact with material causing allergic reaction. It includes poison ivy, chemicals, detergents.

CONTAGION A disease which can be transmitted from one person to another by direct contact.

CONTRACEPTION Prevention of conception and pregnancy. May be mechanical, chemical or by natural body cycle. Also *BIRTH CONTROL.*

CONTUSION See *BRUISE.*

CONVALESCENCE Recovery from a disease or injury. The period in which the recovery takes place.

CONVULSION Violent, uncontrollable spasm of muscles throughout the body. Also *FIT, PAROXYSM.*

CORN An enlarged, inflamed area on a foot caused by pressure or rubbing.

CORONARY ARTERIOGRAPHY An examination in which a radiopaque material is injected into an artery in forearm or groin. X-rays show condition of the coronary (heart) arteries.

CORONARY ARTERY DISEASE Congestion of the arteries nourishing the heart muscles. See *CORONARY THROMBOSIS, ARTERIOSCLEROSIS, INFARCTION.*

CORONARY HEART DISEASE See *CORONARY ARTERY DISEASE.*

CORONARY THROMBOSIS Choking off a branch of the artery feeding the heart muscle by clogging or a clot. Results in heart pain or heart failure. See *ANGINA PECTORIS, ARTERIOSCLEROSIS, INFARCTION.*

CORYZA Head cold. See *COMMON COLD, NASOPHYRANGITIS.*

COUGH Explosive release of air from the lungs to remove irritation from the larger air passages. It is a normal and useful relex action, but during a cold, inflamed mucous membranes may cause coughing without anything to expel.

CRABS Lice affecting the pubic areas.

CRAMP A localized muscle spasm, particularly in leg, foot or abdominal muscles.

CREATININE TEST A test of kidney function. Normal range is less than 1 milligram per 100 milliliters (mg/100 ml).

CREPITUS A crackling sound caused by calcium deposits in joints, particularly knee and neck. Also sound heard through a stethoscope from inflamed lungs. Sometimes used to describe grating sounds from grinding together of the ends of broken bones.

CRETINISM Retardation of mental and physical growth caused by a congenital deficiency of thyroid hormone.

CROHN'S DISEASE See *ILEITIS.*

CROSSED EYES The eye turn inward, toward each other. See *ESOPHORIA, ESOTROPIA, SQUINT, STRABISMUS.*

CROUP A symptom of harsh cough and difficult, wheezing breathing, caused by a number of conditions, such as allergy, bacterial infection or viral infection.

CUBAN ITCH See *SCABIES.*

CURETTAGE A surgical procedure in which injuried or diseased tissue is scraped out of a body cavity. See *D & C.*

CYANOSIS A dark purple discoloration of the skin and mucous membranes from oxygen starvation.

CYCLOPLEGIA A paralysis of the ciliary muscles which dilates the pupils of the eyes, preventing focusing.

CYST A swelling containing fluid, appearing most often in the skin and the ovaries. The word also means "bladder," as in cystitis.

CYSTIC FIBROSIS Hereditary malfunction of several glands, causing severe digestive disorders, breathing difficulties and lung infections, and a tendency to heat stroke. See *MALABSORPTION.*

CYSTITIS Inflammation of a bladder, particularly the urinary bladder, from infection or crystaline deposits. Common symptom is frequent and painful passage of urine.

CYSTOCELE Formation of a pocket in the bladder which does not drain properly. Usually caused by collapse of the uterus after frequent childbearing.

CYSTOGRAPHY An X-ray examination of the urinary bladder using a radiopaque substance introduced with a catheter inserted into the urethra.

CYSTOSCOPY A procedure in which a viewing instrument (cystoscope) is inserted through the urethra into the bladder to inspect for cysts and other problems.

CYSTOURETHROGRAPHY An X-ray examination of the bladder. See *CYSTOGRAPHY.*

D

D & C (DILATION AND CURETTAGE) A surgical procedure involving stretching the opening of the uterus (dilation) and scraping the mucous membrane (curettage).

DANDRUFF A harmless, scaly condition of the scalp. Flakes are visible in hair and on shoulders. More obvious with greasy skin than dry skin. Also *SEBORRHEIC DERMATITIS.*

DEAFNESS Loss of or lack of hearing from many causes. There are three types: 1. defective air conduction, 2. defective bone conduction, and 3. nerve deafness. With age there is often loss of ability to hear high frequencies because of lowered elasticity of the hearing structures.

DEBILITY An overall weakness.

DECONGESTANT A medicine to reduce swolled mucous membranes. See *ANTIHISTAMINE.*

DECUBITUS See *BED SORES.*

DEERFLY FEVER See *TULAREMIA.*

DEGENERATION Deterioration of tissue.

DEHYDRATION Loss of body fluids from lack of water, excessive perspiration or diarrhea.

DELIRIUM TREMENS A condition of withdrawal from alcohol addiction, including sensations of pain, hallucinations, fear.

DELUSION Belief in a non-existant occurance, condition or object.

DEMENTIA Deterioration of mental capacity from brain changes.

DENTIFRICE A material to clean teeth. Also *TOOTHPASTE.*

DEODORANT A preparation to mask or eliminate body odor.

DEPILATORY A preparation to remove hair.

DEPRESSANT A drug to reduce body or mental activity.

DEPRESSION Sad feelings and a lowering of spirits, greater than normal, over a prolonged period. Extreme cases may involve suicide. See *MANIC DEPRESSIVE.*

DERMABRASION Scraping or sanding off outer layers of skin to remove scars and blemishes.

DERMATITIS Non-bacterial inflammation of the skin, often related to an allergy or to contact with irritating materials. Atropic dermatitis is a chronic, mild skin inflammation with a light, patchy rash and an intense itch. Contact dermatitis is an inflammation from an irritating substance. It is often an occupational problem associated with exposure to chemicals. Actinic (solar) dermatitis is caused by exposure to the sun with a more pronounced reaction than in the average person.

DERMOID CYSTS Cysts at corners of eyebrow, skull, root of nose. Attached to the bone. Occur usually in children between 10 and 12 years old.

DETACHED RETINA Detachment of the rear surface of the eye due to a blow or disease.

DEVIATED SEPTUM A malformation of the cartilage which separates the two nasal passages, usually resulting in an inability to breathe normally through one or both sides of the nose.

DEVIL'S GRIP See *PLEURODYNIA.*

DIABETES Abnormal excess of urine. Usually used to mean diabetes mellitus, a deficiency in insulin which prevents the body from regulating the use of sugar. Also, but more rarely, used to mean diabetes insipidus, which results from lack of a pituitary hormone that controls urine production.

DIAGNOSIS An analysis of a patient's condition.

DIALYSIS A blood cleaning process outside the body in an artificial kidney (dialysis machine). Used where the patient has suffered kidney failure.

DIAPER RASH A contact dermatitis caused by prolonged contact with caustic urine or feces. See *CONTACT DERMATITIS, DERMATITIS.*

DIARRHEA Frequent and fluid bowel movements. Usually due to inflammation of the intestines from viruses, bacteria, parasites or allergic reactions to food.

DIATHERMY Electronic heating of body tissue to increase circulation, reduce pain.

DIATHESIS See *HEREDITARY.*

DICK TEST A skin test for immunity to scarlet fever.

DIFFERENTIAL WHITE CELL COUNT A blood test to determine differences in the counts of the six different white cells for leads to the type of infection involved.

DIPHTHERIA An acute bacterial infection of the mucous membranes of the throat. Danger is from toxins produced by the bacteria.

DIPLEGIA Paralysis of both arms or both legs, usually caused by muscle imbalance. See *PARAPLEGIA.*

DIPLOPIA See *DOUBLE VISION.*

DIRECTIONAL DOPPLER ULTRASONOGRAPHY An ultrasonic test of blood flow velocity in neck arteries. See *CAROTID ARTERY TEST.*

DISCHARGE A secretion or flow of liquid.

DISLOCATION Displacement of the moving parts of a joint. Involves tearing of ligaments. Dislocated joints are either immobilized or unstable.

DISKOGRAPHY An X-ray examination to determine abnormality of vertebral disks. Radioactive material is injected into the disk.

DISORIENTATION Mild mental confusion about where or when a person is.

DISTAL Far from the center of the body.

DIURESIS Overactivity of the kidneys, usually induced by drugs. See *DIEURETIC.*

DIURETIC A drug which increases the flow of urine, relieving edema. Also *WATER PILL.* See *EDEMA.*

DIVERTICULITIS Inflammation of a diverticulum (bulge or pouch of the intestines). Chronic diverticulitis has symptoms much like intestinal cancer: constipation, occasional bleeding from the rectum, vague abdominal pain.

DIVERTICULOSIS Occurance of a small pouch or bulge (diverticulum) in the large intestine. Usually harmless and causes no symptoms unless inflamed. Frequently occuring with age.

DIZZINESS A feeling of unsteadiness, of surroundings revolving. See *VERTIGO.*

DONOR One who gives blood or organs.

DOSE See *GONORRHEA.*

DOUBLE VISION A disorder where the eyes do not track together and the brain receives two different images, usually of the same objects, displaced from one another. Usually caused by muscle imbalance, although injury and some drugs may cause the condition. A child with a "squint" may suppress one image, leading to a "lazy" eye. Also *DIPLOPIA.* See *AMBLYOPIA.*

DOUCHE A wash. Usually refers to flushing of the vaginal area.

DOWN'S SYNDROME A congential growth defect with retarded mental and physical growth. The child develops vaguely oriental features, leading to the description "mongoloid." Although requiring special education, such individuals are friendly, cheerful and can generally look after themselves and perform uncomplicated jobs. Also *MONGOLISM.*

DROPSY Excess fluid in the body tissues. A term once used to describe the edema arising from diabetes. Also *ASCITES.* See *EDEMA.*

DROWNING Asphixiation (suffocation) by fluid.

DUODENAL ULCER See *PEPTIC ULCER, ULCER.*

41

DUODENOSCOPY An examination of the duodenum by inserting an endoscope down the throat and through the stomach.

DWARFISM The growth defect which causes abnormally small stature in an adult. See *ACHONDROPLASIA*.

DYSENTERY Infection of the large intestine by either a parasite or bacteria. Often accompanied by pain, straining and mucus.

DYSKESIA See *CONSTIPATION*.

DYSLEXIA Difficulty in reading due to a brain disorder or eye muscle imbalance.

DYSMENORRHOEA Pain accompanying menstrual periods. Usually in the lower abdomen or small of the back. Primary dysmenorrhoea occurs with or following the first period. It usually ends with birth of the first child. Secondary dysmenorrhoea occurs in women who have had earlier, normal periods. It is generally a symptom of some gynecological problem. Also *MENSTRUAL CRAMP*. See *MENSTRUATION*.

DYSPAREUNIA Painful coitus. Primary dyspareunia is an involuntary contraction of vaginal muscles. Secondary dyspareunia is generally a result of inflammation, infection, an inpenetrable hyman, or shrinkage of vaginal lining after menopause.

DYSPEPSIA See *INDIGESTION*.

DYSPHAGIA Extreme difficulty in swallowing, usually due to a spasm of the throat or a blockage.

DYSPNEA Difficulty in breathing; also extreme shortness of breath.

DYSTROPHY Defective development; degeneration. See *DEGENERATION*.

E

ECG See *EKG*.

EKG (ELECTROCARDIOGRAM) An instrument (the electrocardiograph) amplifies minute electrical currents generated by the heart. The tracings on a paper strip are called an electrocardiogram. Also *ECG*.

EEG (ELECTROENCEPHLOGRAM) An instrument (the electroencephlograph) measures minute electrical currents (brain waves) produced by the brain.

EMG (ELECTROMYOGRAM) A test to measure electrical activity of a muscle. Used to determine muscle disease and nerve disease.

ESR (ERYTHROCYTE SEDIMENTATION RATE) A blood test to indicate presence of disease. Measures rate at which red cells settle out of a blood sample. Normal range: Less than 15 millimeters per hour for males under 50; less than 20 millimeters per hour for females under 50; less than 20 ml/h for males over 50; less than 30 ml/h for females over 50.

EAGLE TEST A blood test for syphilis.

EARACHE The ear is very sensitive; earache is caused by a wide range of irritations — inflammation of the Eustachian tube, wax, infection of the eardrum, pimples or boils in the ear canal. See *OTITIS MEDIA*.

ECCHYMOSIS See *BRUISE*.

ECHOCARDIOGRAPHY An examination of the heart by ultrasound (high frequency sound waves).

ECHOENCEPHALOGRAPHY An ultrasound test to locate hemorrhage, blood clots, tumors or fluid in the brain. See *ULTRASOUND*.

ECLAMPSIA Convulsions during pregnancy.

ECTOPIC Out of position organ or body part. Ectopic pregnancy is a fetus in the Fallopian tube.

ECTOPIC PREGNANCY A pregnancy in which the ovum, fertilized in the Fallopian tube, implants itself there instead of descending into the uterus. Seldom lasts more than 2 to 3 months, usually with extreme pain if it lasts longer than 8 weeks. Also *TUBULAR PREGNANCY*.

ECZEMA Allergic skin condition. Symptoms are dry, itching skin. Scratching causes weeping, infected skin. Continued scratching can cause rough, thickened skin. Also *ATOPIC DERMATITIS*. See *ALLERGY*.

EDEMA Collection of fluid in the tissues. Non-localized excess fluid is called dropsy. Mechanical (gravity) edema is caused by lack of circulation, generally from varicosed veins, excessive standing or sitting. It usually affects legs and feet. Osmotic edema is caused by excessive salt in the system, infection, allergy, heart failure, starvation. Also *DROPSY*.

ELECTROCARDIOGRAPH An instrument which records heart action. See *EKG*.

ELECTROENCEPHLOGRAPH An instrument to record electrical activity of the brain. See *EEG*.

ELECTROLYSIS An electric charge used to remove hair.

ELECTRONYSTAGMOGRAPHY A series of tests to determine condition of the sense of balance.

ELECTROOCULOGRAPHY An examination of the retina's sensitivity to light. Also *EOG*.

ELECTRORETINOGRAPHY An examination of the electrical activity of the retina during stimulation by colored lights. Also *ERG*.

ELEPHANTITIS Extreme thickening of the skin due to chronic obstruction of the lymphatic vessels, usually caused by parasitic worms. Also *FILARIASIS*.

ELIMINATION DIET A test for foods suspected of being allergens. Food is eliminated from the diet and reintroduced to discover if allergic reactions occur. See *ALLERGENS, ALLERGY*.

EMBOLISM Blockage of an artery by a clot (embolus). A pulmonary embolism is the result of a clot from a vein lodging in the lungs with attendant localized pneumonia. Occurring in an artery supplying blood to the brain, an embolism causes a stroke. See *STROKE*.

EMBOLUS A blood clot or air bubble blocking an artery. See *EMBOLISM, PHLEBITIS*.

EMETIC A medicine which causes vomiting.

EMESIS See *VOMITING*.

EMOLLIENT A skin softening preparation.

EMPHYSEMA Loss of elasticity and function of lung air vesicles, resulting in lowered lung efficiency.

EMPYEMA An abscess formed by collection of pus in a natural body cavity. Most often used to describe a complication of pleuresy. See *PLEURESY*.

ENCEPHALITIS Inflammation of the brain, usually by a virus. Symptoms include lassitude, an urge to sleep, fever. Also *BRAIN FEVER, SLEEPING SICKNESS*.

ENDEMIC A disease always present in a specific area or portion of the population.

ENDOCARDITIS Inflammation of the lining or valves of the heart. Rheumatic endocarditis is a result of rheumatic fever. See *RHEUMATIC FEVER*.

ENDOMETRITIS Inflammation of the uterus. Also *METRITIS*.

ENDOSCOPY An examination of the esophagus, stomach and duodenum by insertion of an instrument (the endoscope) which provides light and view of the suspected area.

ENEMA A fluid injected into the rectum to clean out the bowel, to administer food or drugs.

ENTERIC FEVER See *TYPHOID FEVER*.

ENTERITIS Inflammation of the intestines from many causes. Gastroenteritis is inflamation of the stomach. See *GASTROENTERITIS, ILEITIS*.

ENURESIS See *BED WETTING*.

EPEDEMIC A disease which appears in an area or a portion of the population, spreads, then disappears.

EPIGLOTITIS Inflammation of the epiglottis. Symptoms are similar to croup, but will not respond to simple remedies. Can seriously interfere with breathing.

EPILEPSY A chronic, functional nervous disorder, usually accompanied by seizures. Gran mal involves unconsciousness and convulsions. Petite mal involves only a fleeting loss of consciousness, and the patient may be unaware anything has happened. Only slight hereditary influence is suspected.

EPISTAXIS See *NOSE BLEEDING*.

EPITHELIOMA Cancer of the skin.

ERYSIPELAS A skin inflammation which creates bright red areas. Also *ST. ANTHONY'S FIRE*.

ERYTHEMA Inflammation (reddening) of the skin.

ERYTHEMA INFECTIOSUM See *FIFTH DISEASE*.

ERYTHEMA INTERTRIGO See *CHAFING*.

ERYTHEMA TOXICUM Flat red splotches appearing on up to half of newborn babies, which disappear after about seven days. Harmless.

ERYTHREDEMA POLYNEUROPATHY Swollen, red eruption of hands and feet of children. There may also be rheumatic-like pains. Also *ACRODYNIA*.

ESOPHAGOSCOPY An examination of the esophagus by inserting an endoscope through the mouth. Also *ENDOSCOPY*.

ESOPHORIA Crossed eyes. See *SQUINT, STRABISMUS*.

ESOTROPIA One eye turns inward. See *SQUINT, STRABISMUS*.

EUNUCH A castrated male; one with testes removed.

EUPHORIA Abnormally elevated spirits, elation.

EXANOPSIA Suppression of the vision in one eye.

EXANTHEM An eruption of the skin.

EXCRETION The passing of waste products.

EXERCISE ELECTROCARDIOGRAPHY See *STRESS TEST*.

EXOPHORIA The eyes turn outward, away from each other. See *SQUINT, STRABISMUS*.

EXOPHTHALMOMETRY An examination of the degree of bulging of the eyes. An instrument visually detects position of the eye in relation to the facial plane.

EXOPHTHALMOS Protruding eyes. Commonly caused by overactive thyroid gland (exophthalmic goiter).

EXOTROPIA One eye turns outward. See *SQUINT, STRABISMUS, WALL EYES*.

EYELID CYSTS See *CHALAZION*.

EYELID NODULES See *XANTHELASMA*.

EYESTRAIN An ache arising from muscular strain. May be caused by poor light (bringing work to close to the eyes to compensate for bad lighting) and uncorrected visual defects. Primarily a binocular (two-eyed) problem.

F

FAINTING Sudden unconsciousness resulting from a reflexive blood pressure drop in the brain. Usually emotional, although it may be caused by medical shock. Also *SYNCOPE*.

FALLING OUT SPELL See *CONVULSION*.

FALSE PREGNANCY See *PSEUDOCYESIS*.

FEBRIL See *FEVER*.

FEEBLEMINDEDNESS Low mental capacity.

FEEBLENESS See *ASTHENIA*.

FELON An infection of the fingertip pad.

FENESTRATION An operation to restore hearing by opening a "window" between the middle and inner ears.

FEVER Elevated body temperatures. Also used to refer to any disease which has fever as a regular symptom. Small children generally react to any infection with an elevated temperature. See *TEMPERATURE*.

FEVER BLISTER See *HERPES SIMPLEX I*.

FIBRILLATION Rapid, uncoordinated heart beat, causing lack of pumping action of the heart. See *ARRHYTHMIA*.

FIBROID A uterine tumor, a fibrous lump which causes excessive bleeding during menstruation, discomfort and sometimes pain. Also *FIBROMYONNA*.

FIBROMA A nonmalignant tumor of fiberous tissue.

FIBROSITIS Muscular pain of undetermined cause. Intermittant in nature. May affect any group of muscles, but found particularly in the back. Tenseness or faulty posture are suspected.

FIFTH DISEASE A viral disease gaining its common

name from its final listing as one of the common contagious rashes of childhood. Symptom is a light red rash characteristic of a "slapped cheek," which appears and disappears during the course of the disease. Also *ERYTHEMA INFECTIOSUM.*

FISHSKIN DISEASE See *ICTHYOSIS.*

FISSURE A furrow, cleft or slit, often of the anus. See *ANAL FISSURE.*

FISTULA An abnormal passage leading from an abscess, cavity or a hollow organ to the surface, or from one organ to another. Most commonly from the rectum to the skin surface. See *ANAL FISTULA.*

FIT An attack of uncoordinated movement: 1. with screaming, tears, threshing of limbs. See *HYSTERIA, TANTRUM.* 2. A jerking of muscles, spasms and rigid contraction. See *EPILEPSY.* Also *ICTUS.*

FLAT FEET A condition in which the normal longitudinal arch of the foot has relaxed, usually placing strain on foot and leg muscles.

FLATULENCE Expelling of intestinal gas from the anus. Results from nervousness or fermentation, particularly during constipation.

FLOATERS Small solid particles in the vitreous of the eye, seen as spots or lines in the vision. Also *MUSCAE VOLITANTES.*

FLUORESCEIN ANGIOGRAPHY An examination to evaluate the blood vessels in the retina. A fluorescent dye is injected into the arm and photographs are made of its passage through the eyes.

FLURODATION Fluoride added to drinking water to inhibit tooth decay.

FOLLICULITIS Inflammation of hair follicles.

FOLLICULITIS BARBAE Inflammation of hair follicles on the face.

FOOD POISONING Usually caused by bacteria, such as *salmonella* or *clostridium botulinum.* Generally accompanied by nausea, vomiting, pain and diarrhea. See *BOTULISM, SALMONELLA.*

FOOTBALL KNEE Detachment or tearing of one or both of the meniscus (half-moon shaped) cartilages on each side of the knee joint, which separate the joint surfaces. A loose meniscus may interfere with the knee motion. Also *TRICK KNEE.*

FRACTURE A break in a bone. A simple fracture is a break without a penetration of the skin. In a compound fracture, the broken bone penetrates muscle and skin to create an open wound. A complicated fracture is where the broken ends penetrate other organs. A comminuted fracture is splintered. A spontaneous fracture is one in an abnormally weak bone, as in osteoporosis. See *OSTEOPOROSIS.*

FRIGIDITY Lack of sexual desire in women.

FROSTBITE Damage by freezing. Affects skin and sometimes underlying tissue with an effect very similar to burning. The safest way to thaw frostbitten skin — usually fingers, toes, ears or nose — is to warm it with blood temperature water. Friction should be avoided.

FRUSTRATION Feeling that results from blocking or interruption of progress toward a goal.

FUNGUS INFECTION Invasion of fungus, a simple form of plant life, which may live upon human skin or tissue. More closely related to bacteria than plants. Also *MYCOSES.* See *RINGWORM, ATHLETE'S FOOT, THRUSH.*

FURNUCLE See *BOIL.*

FUSION Immobilization of a joint by surgery. Commonly used for fixation of vertabrae to alleviate difficulties arising from a ruptured disc (spinal fusion).

G

GI (GASTROINTESTINAL) SERIES An X-ray examination of the upper part of the digestive system. Radiopaque barium "cocktail" is swallowed. See *LOWER GI SERIES.*

GU (GENITOURINARY) EXAMINATION An examination of the genitals and the urinary system.

GALACTOSEMIA Congenital defect which makes some infants show mental deficiency after drinking milk.

GALLBLADDER ATTACK Pain and/or indigestion caused by either inflammation or gall stones. There is usually an intolerance of fatty foods, since fat stimulates the gallbladder. See *GALL STONES.*

GALL STONES Deposits of calcium salts combined with cholesterol, bile pigment or both. May plug bile ducts. See *CALCULUS.*

GAMMA GLOBULIN Given by injection to improve immunity against virus diseases and build resistance to infection. Used especially to immunize against viral hepititis. See *HEPITITIS.*

GANGRENE Death of tissue. Gas gangrene involves badly crushed or torn tissue where bacteria multiply and cause decomposition with formation of a gas that causes a distinctive stench. see *NECROSIS.*

GASTRECTOMY An operation on the stomach.

GASTRIC ULCER See *PEPTIC ULCER, ULCER.*

GASTRITIS Inflammation of the stomach lining. Sometimes due to allergy, but most commonly caused by irritation of alcohol, drugs, tobacco, etc., which cause chemical irritation.

GASTROENTERITIS Inflammation of the stomach lining and intestines, with vomiting, abdominal pain and diarrhea. Usually a virus infection, but may also be caused by bacteria, food poisoning and heavy metal (lead, bismuth) poisoning.

GASTROSCOPY Direct examination of the stomach with a gastroscope introduced through the throat.

GASTROPTOSIS Dropped stomach.

GAZE TEST A test to determine the condition of the sense of balance.

GERMAN MEASLES A common childhood virus disease. Symptoms are fever, swollen lymph nodes and a rash. It is milder than true measles. Incubation after exposure is 2-3 weeks. The infectious state lasts from the day before symptoms appear to the day after they clear up — usually a period of 4-5 days. The disease causes abortion or birth defects if it infects a pregnant woman within the first three months of her pregnancy. Also *RUBELLA*.

GIGANTISM Abnormal growth resulting in height substantially greater than normal as a result of an overactive pituitary gland. See *ACROMEGALY*.

GINGIVITIS A bacterial inflammation of the gums. Untreated, causes loosened teeth which eventually result in their loss.

GLANDULAR FEVER See *MONONUCLEOSIS*.

GLAUCOMA A disease caused by increased fluid pressure, reducing the field of vision. See *TUNNEL VISION*.

GLIOMA A tumor of nerve tissue.

GLOBULIN TEST A blood test to determine the globulin level of the system. High globulin levels may indicate low albumin, parasites or cancer development.

GLOMERULONEPHRITIS A common form of kidney disease in children. It is an allergic reaction to a form of streptococcus bacteria.

GLOSSITIS Inflammation of the tongue surface. Commonly associated with malnutrition or anemia.

GLUCOSE TEST A test for the sugar level in the blood to identify diabetes and hypoglycemia. Normal range is 70 to 110 milligrams per 100 milliliters of blood (mg/100 ml). See *DIABETES, HYPOGLYCEMIA*.

GLUCOSE TOLERANCE TEST A test series to detect early diabetes and other metabolic disorders. Blood and urine levels of sugar are taken after controlled amounts are ingested by the patient.

GLYCOSURIA Excretion of glucose (sugar) into the urine. Usually associated with diabetes.

GOITER Enlargement of thyroid gland due to lack of iodine in the diet (rare today) or tumorous growth, either benign or malignant.

GOLD TREATMENT See *CHRYSOTHERAPY*.

GONIOSCOPY An examination for the cause of glaucoma. A slit lamp inspection for fluid absorption from the eye. See *GLAUCOMA*.

GONORRHEA A common venereal disease due to bacteria which invades mucous membranes through sexual contact. In a man there may be pain and pus. Symptoms are similar in many women, although some have no apparent symptoms at all and are not aware they are infected. Complications include arthritis and eye infection of newborn children.

GONORRHEA TEST A test of the discharge from penis or vagina to check for presence of gonorrhea infection.

GOUT A metabolic dysfunction in which kidneys do not remove uric acid from the blood. When blood levels rise to certain levels, uric acid crystalizes out in the joints, creating gouty arthritis.

GRAND MAL See *EPILEPSY*.

GRANULOCYTOPENIA A lack of leukocytes (white cells) in the blood. Also *AGRANULOCYTOSIS*.

GRANULOMA INGUINALE A bacterial venereal disease marked by ulcers at the point of entry.

GREEN SICKNESS See *CHLOROSIS*.

GREENSTICK FRACTURE Young bones often do not break cleanly but split or splinter like a growing branch. May also happen in certain leg and arm bones at any age.

GRIPPE An outmoded name for influenza. See *INFLUENZA*.

GROWING PAINS Childhood pains formerly attributed to "growing." Now believed to be from muscle strain following vigorous activities. Usually of short duration.

GUMBOIL A bacterial infection at the root of a tooth which breaks through the gum.

GYNECOMASTIA Enlargement of the male breasts. Occurs occasionally in young men temporarily. Frequently found in older men, particularly those overweight.

H

HABITUATION Becoming accustomed to the effects of a medicine or drug so usefulness is inhibited.

HALITOSIS Bad breath.

HALLUCINATION Visual or aural sensations without physical origin. Often called "hearing voices" or "seeing things." May be due to fatigue, fever, drug or alcohol addiction, hysteria or schizophrenia. See *SCHIZOPHRENIA*.

HAMMERTOE A condition where a toe is forced into a bent position with the second joint raised. Usually caused by improperly fitting shoes. More common in women than men.

HANSEN'S DISEASE See *LEPROSY*.

HARDENING OF THE ARTERIES See *ARTERIOSCLEROSIS*.

HARELIP A congenital condition where the upper lip is separated in the center, resembling the lip of a rabbit (hare).

HAYFEVER. A seasonal allergy causing irritation of the nose lining by various plant pollens. Symptoms, which include inflammation of mucous membranes, sneezing, ears and often headaches, are often alleviated by use of antihistamines. Also *ALLERGIC RHINITIS*. See *ALLERGY, ANTIHISTAMINES*.

HEADACHE A symptom of many illnesses, drugs (such as alcohol), high blood pressure, infections, anxiety. Usually responds to mild analgesics. See *SICK HEADACHE, MIGRAINE HEADACHE, ANALGESIC*.

HEART ATTACK A general term covering heart disturbances. See *CORONARY THROMBOSIS, HEART FAILURE, INFARCTION*.

HEARTBURN Indigestion in which gaseous pressures in the stomach and duodenum are forced past the sphincter (valve) at the top of the stomach into the esophagus. Accompanied by a feeling of pressure in the chest, burning and sometimes acute pain, often mistaken for heart pain. Sometimes accompanied by regurgitation of food into the esophagus.

HEART FAILURE Lack of sufficient pumping pressure from the heart, causing poor circulation and an accumulation of fluid in the tissues. See *EDEMA*.

HEART MURMUR Abnormal heart sounds.

HEAT EXHAUSTION See *HEATSTROKE*.

HEAT PROSTRATION See *HEATSTROKE*.

HEATSTROKE Illness from body overheating. Sweating causes loss of salt, resulting in fatigue, cramps, nausea and even loss of consciousness. In humid, hot conditions, fever may exist. Most symptoms disappear when water and salt are administered. Also *SUNSTROKE*.

HEIMLICH MANEUVER A procedure for expelling a foreign object which is choking someone by obstructing the throat. The subject is gripped from behind and a fist is shoved into the diaphragm to cause an involuntary explusion of air, freeing the object.

HELMINTHIASIS Infestation of parasitic worms.

HEMARTHROSIS Bleeding into the joints as a result of hemophilia. See *HEMOPHILIA*.

HEMATEMESIS Vomiting of blood.

HEMATOCRIT TEST A blood test for anemia. Measures volume of red cells in a sample of whole blood. Normal range is 40-54% for males; 36-46% for females.

HEMATOMA Swelling caused by bleeding into tissues. See *BRUISE*.

HEMATURIA Presence of blood (red cells) in the urine as the result of kidney or bladder injury or disease. In males may also be caused by prostate disease.

HEMIPLEGIA Paralysis of one side of the body, usually from a stoke affecting the opposite side of the brain. See *STROKE*.

HEMOGLOBIN LEVEL A blood test for anemia. Measures hemoglobin (red cells) by weight in a sample of blood. Normal range is 14-18 grams per 100 milliliters of blood for males; 12-16 grams per 100 milliliters (g/100 ml) for females.

HEMOPHILIA A hereditary disease where prolonged bleeding occurs from even the smallest injury. Lack of normal clotting factor in the blood is the cause.

HEMOPTYSIS Spitting up blood. May be symptom of tuberculosis or lung cancer. May also be caused by infection or heart disease.

HEMORRHAGE Extensive bleeding.

HEMORRHOIDS A varicosing of the external veins in the anus, causing painful swelling and itching (pruritis). Also *PILES*.

HEPATITIS Inflammation of the liver, usually from virus infection. Serum hepatitis is transmitted through blood or through blood or serum on hypodermic needles used for immunizations or transfusions. Epidemic jaundice is transmitted by human contact or by contamination of food or water. See *JAUNDICE*.

HEREDITARY Inherited from parents. Some conditions run in families (such as tendencies for high blood pressure, some types of cancer, angina, varicose veins,

Tay-Sachs disease, sickle cell anemia, etc.) Also *DIATHESIS*.

HERNIA Penetration of a retaining wall by a part or organ. Most commonly used to describe intestines penetrating the abdominal wall. Inguinal hernia is the common form in men, where intestines pass through the gap where the testes descended into the scrotum. Similar is the femoral hernia where the intestines bulge into the groin where the femoral blood vessels enter the thigh. Diaphragmatic hernia is where the stomach bulges through the diaphragm at the point the esophagus enters the stomach.

HERPES SIMPLEX Type I: A grouping of inflammed blisters caused by a virus attacking subcutaneous nerve endings in lips or surrounding facial skin. The resulting ulcer may take 9 to 14 days to heal, but rarely leaves scarring. The virus stays in the system between attacks. Also *FEVER BLISTER*. Type II is a venereal version of the disease. Blisters occur on or adjacent to genitals. May be painful.

HERPES TEST A blood test for herpes virus.

HERPES ZOSTER A virus disease caused by the same virus that causes chickenpox. Symptoms are fever and painful blisters, generally around the chest or abdomen. Not related to Herpes Simplex. Also *SHINGLES*.

HIVES An allergic reaction. Symptoms are a rash of itchy red bumps. Some causes are drugs, milk, eggs, wheat, chocolate, shellfish, berries, cheese, nuts, pollens, insect bites, pork. May also be emotional in nature. Also *URTICARIA*.

HICCUPS Spasms of the diaphragm muscle, causing the hics. There are thousands of folk remedies, however, physicians use medications to reduce the involuntary spasms.

HIGH BLOOD PRESSURE See *HYPERTENSION*.

HINTON TEST A blood test for syphilis.

HIRSCHSPRUNG'S DISEASE Congenital defect of the large intestine resulting in distention of infant's abdomen.

HOARSENESS Inflammation or irritation of the vocal cords. See *LARYNGITIS*.

HODGKIN'S DISEASE A form of lymphoid cancer accompanied by fever, enlarged lymph nodes and spleen, and dangerously lowered resistance to infection. Also *LYMPADENOMA*.

HONEYMOON CYSTITIS A bladder infection in women after frequent sexual activity.

HOOKWORMS A common parasite infecting the intestinal tract. Incurred through infected soil or by contamination from feces of infected humans or animals.

HORDEOLUM An infection of an eyelash follicle. See *STYE*.

HORMONE A glandular excretion into the blood.

HOT FLASHES See *HOT FLUSHES*.

HOT FLUSHES Feeling of extreme heat, facial burning, perspiration. Usually caused by menopause. Also *HOT FLASHES*.

HUMECTANT A preparation to keep skin moist. Also

MOISTURIZER.

HUNCHBACK See *KYPHOSIS.*

HUNTINGDON'S CHOREA A hereditary condition with symptoms of uncontrolled movements and progressive mental disorder. Symptoms do not appear until adulthood. Also *CHOREA MAJOR.*

HYALINE-MEMBRANE DISEASE See *RESPIRATORY DISTRESS SYNDROME.*

HYATID DISEASE A tapeworm infestation which creates cysts in muscles and internal organs. Usually contracted from food contaminated by dogs or from dog feces.

HYDROCELE Swollen testicles. An edema of the membrane surrounding the testes.

HYDROCEPHALUS Enlargement of the head found in infants. Caused by collection of cerebrospinal fluid in the skull when normal drains are blocked. Also *WATER ON THE BRAIN.*

HYDROPHOBIA A symptom of rabies which means "fear of water," since rabies victims have an inability to swallow fluids and reject them, often violently. See *RABIES.*

HYPERACTIVITY SYNDROME A group of symptoms of other conditions, including excessively increased activity, wide mood changes, easy distractability, explosive outbursts, poor impulse control and frequently with learning difficulties. The child may also be clumsy.

HYPEREMESIS GRAVIDARUM A toxic condition of pregnancy, causing severe vomiting. It is not part of morning sickness. May be treated with drugs or even termination of pregnancy. Cause unknown.

HYPERHIDROSIS Excessive sweating.

HYPEROPIA Farsightedness. The inability of the eyes to focus on close objects. Corrected by glasses or contact lenses.

HYPERPLASIA Excessive growth, usually localized as in enlargement of the thyroid gland (goiter), the breasts during pregnancy, non-tumorous enlargement of the prostate.

HYPERPYREXIA High fever, with temperatures at life-threatening levels.

HYPERSENSITIVE VASCULITIS An inflammation of the small blood vessels caused by allergy.

HYPERTENSION High blood pressure. May arise from infection (secondary hypertension) or a separate disease (essential hypertension) which may be benign with few symptoms or malignant with rapidly escalating symptoms. Hypertension is a major cause of stroke, heart failure and other serious conditions.

HYPERTENSIVE RETINOPATHY A vascular disease of the rentina caused by high blood pressure. See *HYPERTENSION.*

HYPERTROPIA One eye deviates upward.

HYPERTROPHY Excessive growth without cell multiplication, as from exercise of muscles.

HYPERVENTILATION Symptoms of dizziness and spots before the eyes caused by breathing rapidly and deeply in which the body absorbs too much oxygen.

HYPNOTIC A drug used to promote sleep.

HYPNOTISM A diagnostic and pschotherapeutic treatment tool. A patient is placed by the hypnotist into a trance where memory is enhanced, or where the subject is suseptible to suggestion. Used for treatment of phobias and to eliminate undesireable habits. Also *MESMERISM.*

HYPOCHRONDRIA Excessive preoccupation with minor or imaginary ills.

HYPOGLYCEMIA Low blood sugar. May be caused by overproduction of insulin by the pancreas or by liver disease (rare).

HYPOPHORIA One eye deviates downward.

HYPOTENSION Low blood pressure.

HYSTERECTOMY An operation to remove the uterus.

HYSTERIA 1. An anxiety condition of screams, tears and fears. Also *FIT.* 2. A neurotic condition with attendant symptoms of disease often present.

HYSTEROSALPINGOGRAPHY An examination of the Fallopian tubes by introducing a radiopaque material into the uterus and taking X-rays.

I

ICU (INTENSIVE CARE UNIT) A hospital area where seriously ill patients are cared for at maximum levels.

IATROGENIC DISEASE A condition caused by the doctor through side effects from treatment.

ICTERUS See *JAUNDICE.*

ICTHYOSIS An hereditary skin condition marked by dry, scaly surface. Also *FISHSKIN DISEASE.*

ICTUS A sudden attack, as in a stroke or fit.

IDEOPATHIC Cause not known. Literally: self-generated.

IDIOSYNCRASY A peculiarity which marks a person as different.

ILEITIS Inflammation of the lower section of the small intestine (ileum). Also *CROHN'S DISEASE.*

IMMERSION FOOT See *TRENCH FOOT.*

IMMUNIZATION Protection against disease. May be natural or induced. See *VACCINATION.*

IMPACTION 1. Broken bone where ends are jammed together and firmly interlocked. 2. A tooth which is wedged in the jaw and unable to emerge.

IMPETIGO A staphylococcus infection of the skin which is contagious by contact. Most common among children. Marked by red ulcerations of the skin.

IMPOTENCE Inability to perform coitus. In men, a failure to get an erection. In women, a spasm of vaginal muscles preventing insertion. May be psychological or physical in cause.

INCONTINENCE Lack of control of bladder or rectal release.

INDIGESTION A breakdown of normal digestion, marked by pain, discomfort, nausea, flatulence. May arise from physical causes (ulcer, gastritis) or from allergy, overeating, worry, anger, drugs, alcohol, etc. Also *DYSPEPSIA*.

INFANTILE PARALYSIS See *POLIOMYELITIS*.

INFANTILISM A congenital condition in which lack of glandular development produces mental retardation and underdeveloped sex organs.

INFARCTION Blockage of a blood vessel, generally an artery which nourishes an organ. Used primarily to describe coronary artery congestion and death (necrosis) of heart muscle tissue. Also *INFARCT*. See *CORONARY THROMBOSIS*.

INFECTION Inflammation or disease caused by bacteria or viruses.

INFERTILITY Inability to conceive a child. See *STERILITY*.

INFLAMMATION Swelling and local irritation of tissue caused by irritation, injury or infection by bacteria or viruses.

INFLUENZA An epidemic virus infection, usually of the mucous membranes of nose, throat, trachea, bronchi and lungs. Symptoms are fever, headache and weakness. May also affect digestion. Pneumonia may follow as a complication.

INGROWN TOENAILS The corners of a toenail, usually on the large toe, grow into the tissue on each side of the toe. Usually treated by cutting a "V" into the center of the nail to relieve pressure on the corners.

INGUINAL HERNIA Penetration of the intestines through the inguinal wall, an area in the male groin between the abdomen and the scrotum. See *HERNIA*.

INSOMNIA Inability to sleep.

INTERTRIGO A skin irritation where two sweaty areas rub together. Usually affects fat individuals. May be complicated by bacterial infection. See *CHAFING*.

INTESTINAL CRAMP Abdominal pain. May be caused by indigestion, constipation, diarrhea, ileitis. Also occurs when swimming in cold water immediately after ingesting a large meal. Also *ABDOMINAL CRAMP*. See *CRAMP*.

INTESTINAL FLU A viral inflammation of the digestive tract. Symptoms are nausea, vomiting, diarrhea and painful cramps. Often mistaken for food poisoning. Also *STOMACH FLU, VIRAL GASTROENTERITIS*.

INTRAVENOUS CHOLANGIOGRAM An examination of the gall bladder by injecting a radiopaque substance into a vein and taking X-rays.

INTRAVENOUS PYELOGRAPHY An examination of the kidneys, ureters and urinary bladder by injecting radiopaque substance and taking X-rays.

INTUSSUSCEPTION Intestinal blockage because one portion of the intestine is drawn into the next. Found primarily in infants under one year. Often misdiagnosed as colic.

INVOLUTIONAL MELANCHOLIA See *DEPRESSION, MELANCHOLIA*.

IRIDECTOMY An eye operation to relieve glaucoma. A small passage at the edge of the iris is created to allow fluid to circulate from the front of the eye to the back. See *GLAUCOMA*.

IRITIS An inflammation of the iris (colored portion) of the eye.

IRON DEFICIENCY ANEMIA Lack of sufficient red blood cells, caused usually by excessive bleeding. Women between puberty and menopause often suffer from this deficiency. See *ANEMIA*.

ISCHEMIA Insufficient blood supply to the heart, causing angina. See *ANGINA PECTORIS, CORONARY ARTERY DISEASE*.

ITCH A stimulation of nerve endings in the skin. Itching may be temporarily relieved by scratching. Certain drugs also relieve itching. Itch is a name sometimes given to scabies. Also *PRURITIS*.

J

JRA (JUVENILE RHEUMATOID ARTHRITIS) A disease of unknown origin which affects children between six months and 12 years. Most children recover.

JAUNDICE Yellowness of the skin and eyes, caused by bilirubin from bile. Caused by disfunction of the liver, blockage of the bile ducts, hepatitis. Also *ICTERUS*. See *HEPATITIS*.

JOCK ITCH A fungus infection of the pubic area aggravated by moisture and friction. Also *TINEA CRURIS*.

JUNGLE ROT A fungus infection, most frequently of the feet, related to ringworm.

JOINT MOUSE Loose clump of bony material floating in a joint. Usually caused by arthritis or injury. May cause the joint to "lock."

K

KELOID Swelling of fibrous tissue in a scar. Harmless but disfiguring. Found primarily in dark skinned individuals.

KERATITIS Inflammation of the cornea (the clear, transparent tissue over the front of the eye).

KERNICTERUS Severe jaundice in newborn infants caused by an Rh factor incompatability. See *Rh FACTOR*.

KETONE TEST A test of urine for diabetes, starvation and other conditions.

KETOSIS Elevated levels of ketones (acetone and similar chemicals) in the blood, caused by diabetes or starvation. Identified by the odor of acetone on the breath.

KIDNEY STONES Deposits of calcium salts in the kidneys. May pass through to the bladder. See *CALCULUS, NEPHROLITHIASIS*.

KISSING DISEASE See *MONONUCLEOSIS*.

KNOCK KNEES A condition where legs, instead of being straight, come together at the knees.

KOILONYCHIA An iron deficiency condition resulting in thin, concave fingernails.

KRAEUROSIS A progressive skin condition involving shriveling and hardening. May affect genital organs.

KYPHOSIS Forward curvature of the spine. Also referred to in elderly women as "dowager's hump." In extreme cases leads to "hunchback" deformity. Also *STOOPED SHOULDERS.*

L

LDH (LACTIC DEHYDROGENASE) TEST A blood test to verify a heart attack. Elevated levels of this enzyme occur within 24 hours of an attack. Also used for liver disease. Normal range is 100 to 255 microUnits per milliliter (uU/ml).

LACERATION A wound caused by tearing instead of cutting.

LACRIMATION Tearing of the eye. Crying.

LAMENESS Loss of leg function.

LAMINECTOMY An operation to remove a portion of vertebra to expose spinal cord.

LAPAROSCOPY An examination of the interior of the abdominal cavity.

LAPAROTOMY An operation to open the abdomen. Used in exploratory surgery and to deliver babies by Caesarean section.

LARYNGECTOMY An operation to remove the larynx.

LARYNGITIS Inflammation of the larnyx resulting in loss of voice.

LARYNGOSCOPY Examination of the larynx (vocal cords) with an instrument (laryngoscope) which provides light and view.

LAVAGE A medical procedure in which the stomach or other body cavity is washed out.

LAXATIVE A medicine to induce bowel movements. Also *PURGATIVE.*

LEAD POISONING Toxic effects of lead in the body, which cannot secrete the heavy metal. Severe symptoms are abdominal pain, anemia, damage to nerves and brain. Most common form is through lead-containing paint which children chew from furniture, woodwork, etc. Also *PAINTER'S COLIC.*

LEG CRAMPS Spasms of the calf muscles due to over-exercise, lack of circulation or vitamin deficiency. Usually occurs during sleep.

LEPROSY A bacterial disease of skin and nerves which may cause raised blotches and lumps on the skin, also ulcers. It may also cause nerve damage, with deadening of skin sensation and pain, loss of skin color and pain, with eventual crippling.

LEPTOSPIROSIS An infectious jaundice contracted from pigs. Also *SWINEHERDER'S DISEASE.*

LESION A wound, injury or other disturbance of a part of the body, such as abscesses and tumors.

LEUKEMIA Cancer of white blood cells (leukocytes), in which white cells abnormally reproduce and inhibit red cell formation.

LEUKOPLAKIA White patches in the mouth. Also *SMOKER'S PATCHES.*

LEUKORREA Heavy secretion of white mucus from the vagina. Also *THE WHITES.*

LICE See *LOUSE.*

LICHEN A skin disease with raised blotches. May be accompanied by itching.

LINCTUS A syrupy cough medicine. Any medicine to be sipped or licked.

LIPOMA A benign skin tumor composed of fat cells.

LIPOPROTEIN PHENOTYPING A blood test to determine levels of various types of blood fats.

LITHOTOMY An operation to remove stones from the bladder.

LITTLE'S DISEASE See *CEREBRAL PALSY.*

LIVER SPOTS See *CHLOASMA.*

LOBECTOMY An operation to remove one lobe of a lung because of cancer or chronic infection.

LOBOTOMY An operation on the brain to sever the frontal lobes to inhibit violent reactions.

LOCKJAW See *TETANUS.*

LOCOMOTOR ATAXIA See *TABES.*

LOP EARS Ears which stand out abruptly from the head.

LORDOSIS Spinal curvature in which the lower back curves inward toward the stomach. Also *SWAYBACK.*

LOUSE A small insect which lives as a parasite on humans, generally in hairy areas. Also *LICE* (plural).

LOW BACKACHE See *LUMBAGO, BACKACHE.*

LOWER GI SERIES X-ray examination of the colon and rectum. See *BARIUM ENEMA.*

LUDWIG'S ANGINA An abscess of the mouth, usually under the tongue.

LUMBAGO Pain in the small of the back (lumbar area). Persistant and often associated with pain in the leg (sciatica). May be caused by muscle strain or a ruptured vertebral disc. Also *LOW BACKACHE.* See *BACKACHE.*

LUMBAR PUNCTURE A method of taking a sample of cerebrospinal fluid to test for meningitis or other infections. A hollow needle is inserted between two lumbar vertebrae into the spinal canal. Also *SPINAL TAP.*

LUPUS VULGARIS Tuberculosis of the skin. Usually affects the face, with lumps, sores and scars. Sometimes mistaken for leprosy.

LUPUS ERYTHEMATOSUS A chronic, non-tubercular skin disease marked by red, scaling blotches on exposed face, scalp and hands. See *XERODERMA.*

LUXATION Dislocation of a joint.

LYMPHADENOMA See *HODGKIN'S DISEASE.*

LYMPHANGIOGRAM An X-ray test for cancer of the lymph system. A radiopaque substance is injected into a lymphatic vessel. Also *LYMPHOGRAPHY.*

LYMPHANGITIS Infection of lymph vessels. See

BLOOD POISONING.

LYMPHOGRANULOMA VENEREUM A tropical virus venereal disease with enlargement of lymph nodes in the groin. There is coarsening and ulceration of the surrounding skin.

LYMPHOGRAPHY See *LYMPHANGIOGRAM.*

LYMPHOMA A tumor of the lymph glands.

LYSIS Gradual lowering of a fever.

M

MACROSCOPIC Able to be seen with the naked eye.

MACULE A skin spot which is not raised above the surrounding area.

MADURA FOOT See *MYCETOMA.*

MALABSORPTION Inability to utilize food values from the diet. Results in malnutrition. See *CARBOHYDRATE INTOLERANCE, CYSTIC FIBROSIS.*

MALADY An illness or disability.

MALAISE A feeling of general discomfort which often precedes an infection.

MALARIA A parasitic infection of the blood, spread by mosquitos. Symptoms are head ache, shivering and fever for a few hours to a day or longer. Repeated on a cyclic basis. Results in anemia.

MAL DE MER See *MOTION SICKNESS.*

MALE PAP TEST See *PROSTATIC ACID PHOSPHATASE TEST.*

MALIGNANT Progressive or terminal condition.

MALINGERING Intentionally feigning an illness or disability. Usually to avoid responsibilities, to gain sympathy or to obtain monetary settlements.

MALNUTRITION Deficiency of any essential food element. Caused by improper diet or illness. See *MALABSORPTION.*

MALOCCLUSION Faulty meeting of the teeth, interfering with the bite.

MALTA FEVER See *BRUCELLOSIS.*

MALUNION Improper alignment in a healed bone.

MAMMOGRAPHY An X-ray of the breast at low radiation levels to detect tumors.

MANIA Uncontrollable excitement caused by mental disturbance. See *MANIC-DEPRESSIVE.*

MANIC-DEPRESSIVE PSYCHOSIS A severe mental disturbance where the mood swings violently between mania — with boundless energy, chattering, high spirits and irrepressible optimism about plans and projects — and depression — with sadness, melancholy, anxiety, retreat from relationships, lack of initiative, even suicide. Subject may be normal between attacks.

MANIPULATION 1. Setting broken bones. 2. Replacement of dislocated joints. 3. Replacement of displaced joints. Practiced by osteopaths and chiropractors to relieve pain.

MANTOUS TEST See *TUBERCULIN SKIN TEST.*

MARAMUS A wasting condition caused by continued malnutrition.

MARCH FRACTURE A break in one of the foot's metatarsal bones, usually caused by unaccustomed exertion, such as jumping or jogging.

MASTECTOMY An operation in which the breast is removed because of cancer. Radical mastectomy is removal of the pectoral muscles and the lymph nodes under the arm. The lumpectomy is the removal of lumps from the breast tissue.

MASTER'S TWO-STEP An exercise in which a subject climbs up and down a two-step high platform before an electrocardiogram is made.

MASTITIS Inflammation of the breast. Generally occurring during nursing, as bacteria infect a cracked nipple.

MASTOIDITIS Inflammation of the mastoid bone which lies behind the ear.

MEASLES A common virus disease spread by airborne droplets. Highly contagious. Symptoms are fever, running nose and eyes, then a sore throat. Finally red spots with white centers appear in the mouth. Two or three days later a red, blotchy skin rash appears on the face and chest. The attack lasts about a week. Vaccine is effective to prevent the disease. Also *MORBILLI, RUBEOLA.*

MECONIUM Greenish bile and mucus passed shortly after birth by infants. Normal.

MAGACOLON See *HIRSCHSPRUNG'S DISEASE.*

MELANCHOLIA Also *INVOLUTIONAL MELANCHOLIA.* See *DEPRESSION.*

MELANOMA A mole; a pigmented tumor; a type of cancer.

MENARCHE The first menstruation at puberty. See *MENSTRUATION.*

MENIERE'S SYNDROME (DISEASE) A recurring disturbance of the middle ear, involving balance and hearing. Symptoms are hissing or ringing sounds in the ear, unsteadiness and sometimes dizziness, nausea.

MENINGIMUS Stiff neck, often at beginning of a cold or influenza attack.

MENINGITIS Inflammation of the meninges, a plastic-like covering protecting the brain and spinal cord. May be mild or severe, often leading to death.

MENOPAUSE Permanent termination of the menstrual cycle. May occur between late 30s and early 50s and may be sudden or gradual in onset. Symptoms experienced by some women are hot flushes, heart palpatations and inflamed vaginal lining. Also *CHANGE OF LIFE, CLIMACTERIC.* See *HOT FLUSHES.*

MENSTRUATION Regular, periodic bleeding from the vagina of women of childbearing age. Caused by shedding and regeneration of the uteral lining. Cycle is from 3 to 5 weeks, and may vary in the same person. Sometimes accompanied by pain. See *DYSMENORRHEA.*

MENSTRUAL CRAMP See *DYSMENORRHEA.*

MENTAL BLOCK Temporary inability to remember or think of something specific.

MENTAL DEFICIENCY Lowered mental capability. Also *FEEBLEMINDEDNESS*.

MESMERISM See *HYPNOTISM*.

METABOLISM The body's fuel conversion mechanism, as food is converted into energy and waste products are broken down for elimination.

METASTASIS Spreading of an infection or cancer from its point of origin throughout the body.

METEORISM Distention of the intestine by gas, accompanied by pain and violent flatulence. See *FLATULENCE*.

METORRHAGIA Uterine hemorrhage.

METRITIS An inflammation of the uterus lining. Also *ENDOMETRITIS*.

MICROCEPHALY Incomplete growth of the head, with undeveloped brain and mental deficiency. Also *PINHEAD*.

MICROSCOPIC URINALYSIS An examination of urine for presence of infection, degeneration or stones in the kidneys.

MICTURITION Urination.

MIGRAINE HEADACHE A common type of headache which generally attacks only one side of the head. Usually preceded by flickering lights (auras), loss of visual areas and nausea. Exact cause unknown. Generally unaffected by usual analgesics.

MILIARIA See *PRICKLY HEAT*.

MILIARY TUBERCULOSIS Tuberculosis infection which is spread widely in small localized sites.

MIOSIS Contraction of the pupil of the eye.

MISCARRIAGE Expulsion of the fetus from the uterus during the fourth, fifth or sixth month of pregnancy.

MITE A small parasitic insect which burrows into the skin and causes an itching irritation. See *SCABIES*.

MITRAL TENOSIS A condition where the mitral valve in the heart is narrowed by scarring from infection. The valve restricts blood flow and leaks. Usual cause is rheumatic fever. See *RHEUMATIC FEVER*.

MITTELSCHMERZ Pain midway between mentrual periods. Accompanies ovulation.

MOLE A pigmented area, often raised in the skin. Also *NEVUS*. See *MELANOMA*.

MONGOLISM See *DOWN'S SYNDROME*.

MONILIASIS A non-venereal vaginal fungus infection. Also *CANDIDA*.

MONONUCLEOSIS A contagious virus disease which infects the lymph nodes (glands). Symptoms include enlarged neck glands, sore throat, nausea, exhaustion. The feeling of weakness may last long after the attack is over. Also *GLANDULAR FEVER, KISSING DISEASE*.

MORBILLI See *MEASLES*.

MORNING SICKNESS A commonly occuring nausea in the early stages of pregnancy. It usually clears up in a few weeks.

MOTILITY STUDIES A test for digestive rate, involving a tube inserted down the throat into the stomach.

MOTION SICKNESS Nausea caused by motion disturbance of the middle ear. It may be incurred by travel in autos and aircraft, but is most common on boats and ships. Also may occur on swings or carousels. Also *AIRSICKNESS, CARSICKNESS, MAL DE MER, SEASICKNESS*.

MOUNTAIN SICKNESS Headache caused by lack of oxygen, usually at 10,000 feet or higher. Symptoms are headache, lassitude, irritability, shortness of breath, dizziness. Also *ALTITUDE SICKNESS*.

MUCUS A clear, viscous liquid which protects the mucous membranes. Often stimulated by over production and thickening by inflammation and infections. Also *PHLEGM*.

MULTIPLE SCLEROSIS A progressive degenerative disease of the central nervous system. Symptoms often mimic other nervous system disorders. There are often spontaneous remissions for varying periods, but progress is generally progressive.

MUMPS A common virus disease spread by airborne droplets. Symptoms are fever, painful swelling of the salivary glands in the neck. Mumps in grown men may cause sterility by infecting the testes. Immunity is gained by having the disease in childhood, where the disease is mild.

MUSCAE VOLITANTES Floating spots in the vision, caused by eyestrain, irritation and disease.

MUSCLE CRAMP A spasm of muscle fibers which is involuntary and painful. Most common in the leg or foot. See *LEG CRAMP*.

MUSCLE RELAXANT A drug to relax muscle spasms.

MUSCULAR ATROPHY Shrinking or wasting away of muscle tissue. May be caused by infection, degenerative disease or disuse. Also *MYOPATHY*.

MUSCULAR DYSTROPHY A degenerative muscle disease in which muscles waste away. Cause is not known. Also *MYOPATHY*.

MYASTHENIA GRAVIS A defective nerve stimulation of the muscles; severe muscular weakness. Also *MYOPATHY*.

MYCOSIS A fungus infection.

MYCETOMA A parasitic infection of the feet caused by mycetes. Also *MADURA FOOT*.

MYELITIS A suffix meaning inflammation.

MYELOGRAM An examination of the spinal column by injecting radiopaque substance and taking X-ray pictures.

MYELOMA Cancer of the bone marrow.

MYIASIS A parasitic infection caused by fly larvae.

MYOCARDIAL INFARCTION See *INFARCTION*.

MYOPATHY Any muscle disease. See *MUSCULAR DYSTROPHY, MYASTHENIA GRAVIS, MYOTONIA*.

MYOPIA Nearsightedness. The inability of the eyes to

focus on distant objects. Corrected by glasses or contact lenses.

MYOSITIS Inflammation of the muscles.

MYOTONIA Abnormal tensing of muscles at rest. Also *MYOPATHY*.

MYRINGOTOMY An operation to open the eardrum to release pus from the middle ear.

MYXEDEMA Skin thickening as a result of low thyroid activity.

N

NPN (NONPROTEIN NITROGEN) A laboratory procedure which tests blood for kidney function.

NAIL BITING See *ONYCHOPHAGIA*.

NARCOLEPSY Uncontrollable sleep, usually for short periods.

NASOPHARYNGITIS Inflammation of the mucous membranes of the nose and throat, usually caused by the common cold. See *COMMON COLD*.

NAUSEA A sensation of being about to vomit.

NEAR SIGHTEDNESS See *MYOPIA*.

NEEDLE BIOPSY A sample of tissue, usually from an organ or a growth, taken by insertion of a hollow needle.

NEOPLASM See *CANCER, TUMOR*.

NEPHRECTOMY An operation to remove a kidney. The body can operate satisfactorily with only one kidney functioning.

NEPHRITIS Inflammation of the kidneys from infection. See *BRIGHT's DISEASE*.

NEPHROBLASTOMA See *WILMS' TUMOR*.

NEPHROLITHIASIS Kidney stones.

NEPHROSIS Degeneration of the kidneys.

NERVOUSNESS A feeling of uneasiness or agitation.

NEURALGIA Nerve pain, as in sciatica. See *SCIATICA*.

NEURASTHENIA Nervous exhaustion. Also *PSYCH-ASTHENIA*.

NEURITIS Inflammation of a nerve.

NEUROMA A nerve tumor.

NEUROSIS A mental disturbance in which the subject generally is aware that something is wrong; an emotional disorder.

NEVUS See *ANGIOMA*.

NITS Tiny white clusters of louse eggs, usually attached to the base of hair strands. See *LOUSE*.

NOMO Serious mouth infection associated with malnutrition. Also *CANCRUM ORIS*.

NOSE BLEEDING Blood from the nose may be caused by injury, fever, high blood pressure or irritation. Also *EPISTAXIS*.

NOSTRUM A medicine with secret ingredients; a quack medicine of no value.

NYCTALOPIA See *NIGHT BLINDNESS*.

NYSTAGMUS An involuntary eye movement associated with disruptions in the sense of balance.

O

OBESITY Overweight; fat; usually weights 15% or more above normal for build. Also *ADIPOSIS*.

OCCLUSION Blockage of a passage, such as a blood vessel.

OCCLUSIVE VASCULAR PAIN Pain from red blood cells blocking capillaries. See *SICKLE CELL ANEMIA*.

OCULOPLETHYSMOGRAPHY A test to measure changes in volume of the eye. See *CAROTID ARTERY TEST*.

OLD AGE See *SENESCENCE*.

OLIGOARTICULAR ARTHRITIS A form of juvenile rheumatoid arthritis which affects less than four joints, but with the danger of eye inflammation. May cause blindness. See *JUVENILE RHEUMATOID AR-THRITIS*.

ONYCHIA Infection under the fingernail.

ONYCHOPHAGIA Nail biting.

OPIATE A narcotic; a drug that dulls sensation; a drug derived from opium; a sedative.

OPISTHOTONOS Muscle spasm which causes the back to ache.

OPTHALMIA See *CONJUNCTIVITIS*.

OPHTHALMIA NEONATORUM Conjuctivitis in newborn infants. Damaging unless treated early. See *CON-JUCTIVITIS*.

OPTHALMASCOPE An instrument for inspecting the inside of the eye. Used for identifying diabetes, Bright's disease, high blood pressure, eye diseases and concussion.

OPTHALMODYNAMOMETRY A test to measure blood pressure in the arteries of the retinas of the eyes. See *CAROTID ARTERY TESTS*.

OPTIC ATROPHY Degeneration of the optic nerve.

OPTOKINETIC TEST A test of balance. A striped drum is revolved to determine if watching it creates eye movements associated with lack of balance. See *NYSTAGMUS*.

ORAL CHOLECYSTOGRAPHY X-rays of the gallbladder after the patient swallows radiopaque dye tablets.

ORCHIDECTOMY An operation to remove the testes.

ORCHIOPEXY An operation to bring down an undescended testicle.

ORCHITIS Inflammation of the testicles. May be caused by mumps or gonorrhea.

ORNITHOSIS A disease transmitted by birds. See *PSITTACOSIS*.

ORTHODONTICS A branch of dentistry which treats teeth irregularities, particularly alignment and "bite."

ORTHOPNEA Inability to breathe lying down.

ORTHOPTICS Training of eye muscles, particularly to correct strabismus. See *STRABISMUS*.

OSTEITIS Inflammation of the bone. See *PAGET'S DISEASE, OSTEOMYELITIS.*

OSTEITIS FIBROSA A form of renal osteodystrophy in which the bone becomes filled with fiberous tissue. See *RENAL OSTEODYSTROPHY.*

OSTEOARTHRITIS Joint degeneration, generally as a result of aging. Includes loss of cartilage and formation of calcium deposits.

OSTEOCHONDROSIS Malformed bone growth. See *PERTHES' DISEASE, SCHLATTER'S DISEASE.*

OSTEOMA Benign bone tumor.

OSTEOMALACIA Bone softening from lack of vitamin D.

OSTEOMYELITIS Bone infection with bone marrow abscesses.

OSTEOPOROSIS Weakening of the bones through loss of calcium. Most common in old age. Women are more prone to condition than men. May also be caused by prolonged corticosteroid treatment.

OSTEOSARCOMA Bone cancer.

OTITIS EXTERNA Inflammation of the skin of the ear canal by fungus or bacteria.

OTITIS INTERNA Inflammation of the inner ear as a complication of otitis media or meningitis. See *OTITIS MEDIA* and *MENINGITIS.*

OTITIS MEDIA Infection of the middle ear, with pus forming to create pressure. May perforate the eardrum or penetrate into the mastoid bone behind the ear.

OTOSCLEROSIS Formation of excess bone in the inner ear. May interfere with hearing.

OTOSCOPE An instrument to inspect the ear canal and ear drum. It shines a light and provides a magnified view of the ear.

OZENA Atrophy of nasal mucous membranes. Associated with crusting and foul odor.

P

PBI (PROTEIN-BOUND IODINE) TEST A test of basal metalolic rate. See *BASAL METABOLISM.*

pH TEST A test to determine degree of acidity or alkalinity of urine.

PKU (PHENYLKETONURIA) Congenital body chemistry defect causing retardation unless corrected early.

P.O. An abbreviation of the latin per os (by mouth).

PZI (PROTAMINE-ZINC INSULIN) A long acting insulin for diabetes control.

PACEMAKER An electrical instrument which delivers a small electric shock to even out heartbeat in certain types of heart disease.

PAGET'S DISEASE 1. Bone deformation, particularly in elderly men. Areas affected are head and leg bones. Deafness is often associated with the condition. 2. Cancer of the nipple.

PAINTER'S COLIC See *LEAD POISONING.*

PALLATIVE Treatment to relieve symptoms instead of underlying disease; a medicine to relieve symptoms.

PALPATATION Heavy or fluttering heart beats felt by the individual.

PALPATION Feeling by hand to determine condition of organs or body parts.

PALSY See *PARKINSON'S DISEASE.*

PANCREATITIS Inflammation of the pancreas.

PANDEMIC An outbreak of disease much wider-spread than an epidemic.

PAPILLOMA See *WART.*

PAP TEST A test (Papanicolasu smears) of cervical scrapings to detect cancer or other disorders of the cervix or uterus.

PARACENTESIS Drainage of fluid from the body by insertion of a tube.

PARAESTHESIA Sensation of tingling, "pins and needles," from nerve irritation or pressure.

PARALYSIS Loss of ability to move muscles, caused by injury or by injury or disease of nerve supply. See *PARESIS.*

PARALYSIS AGITANS See *PARKINSON'S DISEASE.*

PARANOIA A mental disorder with delusions of grandeur and persecution. Often accompanies schizophrenia.

PARAPLEGIA Paralysis of the lower limbs, often from spinal cord injury or disease. Also *DIPLEGIA.*

PARATYPHOID FEVER An infectious, mild, typhoid-like disease.

PARESIS Slight or partial paralysis. See *PARALYSIS.*

PARESTHESIA Burning or tingling of the skin without obvious cause.

PARKINSON'S DISEASE Spasmodic, rhythmic twitching of muscles with poor muscular coordination; a brain affliction. Also *PALSY.*

PAROTITIS Inflammation of the parotid glands. See *MUMPS.*

PAROXYSM See *FIT, CONVULSION.*

PARROT FEVER See *PSITTACOSIS.*

PARTURITION Giving birth.

PATCH TEST A skin contact test for allergy. Tape containing test material is applied to the skin.

PELLAGRA Malnutrition due to niacin (a B vitamin) deficiency. Symptoms are eczema, sore tongue, diarrhea and spinal pain.

PELVIC EXAMINATION An examination of the female sexual organs. An instrument (speculum) is used to open the vagina for visual examination.

PELVIMETRY Measurement of the pelvis before childbirth.

PEMPHIGUS A group of skin diseases marked by development of blisters, itching and pigmented scars.

PEPTIC ULCER A sore; an erosion of a small area of the lining of the stomach (gastric ulcer), or of the duodenum (duodenal ulcer).

PERFUSION Injection of drugs to combat cancer. See *CHEMOTHERAPY*.

PERFUSION TEST A test to determine reaction of the digestive tract by introducing materials through a tube run down the subject's throat.

PERICARDIOCENTESIS A test to determine residual effect of certain diseases on the heart by removing fluid from the membrane around the heart.

PERICARDITIS Inflammation of the sheath around the heart (pericardium).

PERIDONTAL DISEASE Disease of the gums. See *GINGIVITIS, PYORRHEA*.

PERIDONTICS The branch of dentistry which treats gum diseases.

PERIDONTITIS See *GINGIVITIS*.

PERIDONTOSIS Shrinking of the bone surrounding the teeth, causing loosening.

PERITONITIS Inflammation of the peritoneum (abdominal lining). Caused by infection, most commonly from a burst appendix, but also from tuberculosis or a perforated intestine.

PERITONSILLAR ABSCESS An abscess of the tonsils. Also *QUINSY*.

PERLECHE Cracks and inflammation at the corners of the mouth, most often associated with a shortage of B vitamins.

PERNICIOUS ANEMIA Anemia in adults caused by lack of stomach and liver secretion. Also *ADDISONIAN ANEMIA, ANEMIA, PRIMARY ANEMIA*. See *ACHLORHYDRIA*.

PERTHES' DISEASE Malformation of the hipbone. A condition of childhood, more common in boys. See *OSTEOCHRONDROSIS*.

PERTUSSIS See *WHOOPING COUGH*.

PES CAVUS Abnormally high arches of the feet.

PES PLANUS See *FLAT FEET*.

PESSARY A vaginal suppository.

PETIT MAL See *EPILEPSY*.

PHANTOM LIMB An illusion that an amputated limb is still attached and frequently itches or has pain.

PHARINGITIS Inflammation of the pharynx, the area around the soft palate.

PHARYNGOLARYNGOSCOPY Examination of the nose and nasopharynx with an instrument (pharyngolaryngoscope).

PHIMOSIS An abnormally tight foreskin.

PHLEBITIS See *THROMBOPHLEBITIS*.

PHLEBOTOMY Withdrawal of blood from a vein.

PHLEGM See *MUCUS*.

PHOBIA A neurosis with symptoms of anxiety caused by specific objects or situations; a fear. See *ANXIETY*.

PHONOCARDIOGRAPHY A visual record of the heartbeat, taken by an instrument strapped onto the subject's chest.

PHOTOPHOBIA Intolerance to light. Caused by eye inflammation, meningitis, dilation of pupils.

PHOTOSENSITIVITY Sensivity of the skin to sunlight.

PHTHISIS Wasting and emaciation, usually associated with pulmonary tuberculosis. Consumption. See *TUBERCULOSIS*.

PICA A hunger to eat dirt or other unsuitable substances. Found often in small children.

PILES See *HEMORRHOIDS*.

PINHEAD See *MICROCEPHALY*.

PINK EYE An inflammation of the white part (sclera) of the eye. See *CONJUNCTIVITIS, TRACHOMA*.

PLACEBO An inactive substance given as a remedy in order to please a patient.

PLAGUE A ratborne disease. See *BUBONIC PLAGUE, PNEUMONIC PLAGUE*.

PLANTAR WARTS Warts on the sole of the foot.

PLATELET COUNT A blood test for blood clotting ability. A microscopic count of platelets. Normal range is from 140,000 to 400,000 platelets per cubic millimeter of blood smear.

PLETHYSMOGRAPHY A measurement of blood flow through a single artery or vein.

PLEURISY Inflammation of the pleura, the sheath of membrane around the lungs. Dry pleurisy is painful when coughing or breathing. Pleurisy with effusion has fluid between lung and chest wall and is less painful.

PLEURODYNIA Pain spasm in the muscles of the chest. Also *BORNHOLM'S DISEASE, DEVIL'S GRIP*.

PNEUMOCONIOSIS A lung disease caused by inhaled substances. Includes silicosis (silica), asbestosis (asbestos), farmer's lung (fungus mold) and hysisinosis (cotton dust).

PNEUMOENCEPHALOGRAPHY An X-ray examination to detect blood clots, tumors, abscesses, etc., in the brain. Air is injected into the spine.

PNEUMONIA Inflammation of the lungs from infection, with associated fluid collection. Most common is lobar pneumonia, which is inflammation of an entire lobe of the lung. May be caused by either bacteria or viruses.

PNEUMONIC PLAGUE A ratborne disease which attacks the lungs. Symptoms include a grey-blue complexion. See *PLAGUE*.

PNEUMOTHORAX Air in the pleural cavity, imparing respiration. Caused by lung disease or a penetrating wound of the chest.

POISON IVY 1. A wild climbing vine. 2. Skin irritation from contact with toxic oils of the plant. Similar toxic plants are Poison Oak and Poison Sumac.

POLIOMYELITIS A virus infection of the spinal cord, resulting in paralysis, generally of the lower limbs. Vaccines are available.

POLYARTICULAR ARTHRITIS A form of juvenile rheumatoid arthritis most likely to lead to crippling. See *JUVENILE RHEUMATOID ARTHRITIS*.

POLYCYTHEMIA An excess of red blood cells. Found

in people who live at high altitudes, caused by prolonged oxygen shortage.

POLYDACTYLISM Extra fingers or toes.

POLYMASTIA More than two breasts.

POLYNEURITIS Inflammation of many nerves in the body.

POLYP A harmless tumor of the mucous membranes. Found in intestines, nose and uterus.

PORT WINE STAIN See *BIRTHMARK*.

POST MORTEM See *AUTOPSY*.

POST NASAL DRIP Mucus which drips (runs) down the back of the throat. Some drip is normal. In cases of chronic sinusitis or rhinitis, the mucus flow is greater and may have an odor.

POTT'S DISEASE Paralysis of the legs from spinal tuberculosis.

POULTICE A wet dressing for inflamed areas to reduce them by increasing blood circulation.

POX An eruption with pustules.

PRECANCEROUS Advance signs of developing cancer, such as chronic sores and irritations, changing state of moles.

PREMENSTRUAL TENSION Symptoms arising several days before menstrual period. Hormone activity causes the body tissues to hold excess water and salt, resulting in discomfort and irritability. Relieved with diuretic drugs (water pills).

PRESBYCUSIS Loss of hearing with age, particularly in the higher frequencies, which affects distinguishing consonants, although vowel sounds are not affected.

PRESBYOPIA Decreased ability of the eyes, with age, to focus on near objects and printed material.

PRICKLY HEAT Itchy rash with tiny blisters, caused by blockage of sweat glands. Also *MILIARIA*.

PRIMARY ANEMIA See *PERNICIOUS ANEMIA*.

PROCTOSCOPY An examination of the rectum and part of the lower bowel with an instrument (proctoscope) which is inserted into the anus to provide light and a view.

PROGERIA A metabolic disorder which results in rapid aging, particularly of children.

PROGNOSIS A prediction of the future course of a condition or illness.

PROLAPSE Displacement of an organ. A common prolapse in children is of the rectum, where a portion of the large intestine will protrude through the anus. Women who have borne a number of children may have prolapse of the uterus.

PROPHYLAXIS Prevention of disease. Immunization is a prophylaxis.

PROSTATIC ACID PHOSPHATASE A blood test to check for cancer of the prostate. Also *MALE PAP TEST*.

PROSTHESIS An artificial substitute for a part of the body.

PROSTHODONTICS The branch of dentistry which

treats malformation of teeth with prosthetic appliances. See *PROSTHESIS*.

PROSTITIS Inflammation of the prostate gland in men. Symptoms are an urge to urinate frequently, inability to empty the bladder, low back pain.

PROTHROMBIN TIME A blood test for time of clotting. Used when anti-clotting drugs are administered. Also *PROTIME*.

PROXIMAL Close to the center of the body.

PRURITIS See *ITCH*.

PRURITIS ANI Itching of the area around the anus, generally associated with hemorrhoids.

PSEUDOCYESIS False pregnancy. Symptoms of pregnancy seem real, but cause is usually emotional.

PSITTACOSIS A disease transmitted by birds in the parrot family: parrots, budgerigars (parakeets). Causes a type of pneumonia. Also *ORNITOSIS, PARROT FEVER*.

PSORIASIS A chronic skin condition with scaling and red, blotchy patches, sometimes accompanied by intense itching. May be periodic in nature.

PSCHASTHENIA See *NEURASTHENIA*.

PSYCHONEUROSIS See *NEUROSIS*.

PSYCHOPATH An individual with aggressive, antisocial behavior.

PSYCHOSIS Mental illness, loss of touch with reality.

PSYCHOSOMATIC A disease of emotional cause, although symptoms are quite real.

PSYCHOTHERAPY Treatment of mental disorders.

PSYCHOTIC Exhibiting evidence of psychosis. See *PSYCHOSIS*.

PTERYGIUM A white, opaque tissue forming over the cornea, usually caused by repeated irritation from wind and dust.

PTOMAINE POISONING Poisoning from food attacked by bacteria.

PTOSIS Drooping of the upper eyelid.

PUBERTY Beginning of sexual maturity, fertility. Start of adolescence.

PUERPERAL FEVER Infection of the female sex organs following childbirth. Also *CHILDBED FEVER*.

PUERPERAL PYREXIA See *PUERPERAL FEVER*.

PULLED ELBOW Partial dislocation of the elbow, often from pulling small children along behind a parent for an hour or so. Symptoms are inability to lift the arm, with palm facing toward the floor or toward the body.

PULMONARY EDEMA A collection of fluid in the lungs as a result of heart failure. See *HEART FAILURE*.

PULMONARY EMBOLISM A clot of blood lodged in the lung or in the pulmonary arteries. See *EMBOLISM*.

PULMONARY FUNCTION TEST A measurement of breathing difficulties by the subject breathing through a mouthpiece connected to a measuring instrument.

PULSE Regular throbbing in the arteries, caused by heart contractions.

PURGATIVE See *LAXATIVE.*

PURPURA Spontaneous bruising. See *BRUISE.*

PUS A fluid product of inflammation. Contains white blood cells and the debris of dead cells. Usually yellow. May have an odor.

PUSTULE A small blister filled with pus; a pimple. See *PUS.*

PYELITIS Inflammation of the kidneys from infection.

PYELONEPHRITIS Inflammation of the kidneys.

PYELOPHRITIS See *PYELITIS.*

PYEMIA Bacterial infection which causes pus in the blood.

PYLORIC STENOSIS Congenital narrowing of the stomach outlet in newborn infants. Results in vomiting with great force (projectile vomiting).

PYORRHEA A gum infection in the mouth. Also *PERIDONTAL DISEASE.*

PYREXIA See *FEVER.*

Q

Q FEVER An infectious disease carried by ticks. Accompanied by pneumonia.

QUARANTINE Isolation of a person with an infectious disease, usually smallpox, typhus, scarlet fever and yellow fever.

QUINSY An abscess around a tonsil. See *PERITONSILLAR ABSCESS, TONSILITIS.*

R

RAIU (RADIOACTIVE IODINE UPTAKE) A test to determine the condition of the thyroid gland.

RBC (RED BLOOD CELL COUNT) A blood test. A microscopic count of red blood cells.

Rh INCOMPATIBILITY When a baby has a different Rh (rhesus) factor from a mother who has developed antibodies against the opposite factor. The baby is often stillborn, or with profound anemia, severe jaundice. Treatment for anemia and jaundice is an exchange transfusion in which the baby's entire blood supply is replaced with the proper Rh factor blood.

RABBIT FEVER See *TULAREMIA.*

RABIES A virus infection transmitted by bite of an infected animal. Vaccination is effective. See *HYDROPHOBIA.*

RACHITIS See *RICKETS.*

RADIATION POISONING Overdosages of radiation from X-rays and radioactive materials may, in small doses, cause sterility, cancer and birth defects. Larger doses cause cellular destruction similar to burning.

RADIOACTIVE SCAN An examination of various organs by introducing radioactive tracer doses of isotopes combined with chemicals attracted to specific organs. The area is then scanned by special instrumentation.

RADIOLOGY X-ray examination.

RALE An abnormal lung sound, usually from moisture in the lungs.

RASH A skin eruption.

RAYNAUD'S DISEASE Spasm of small arteries in hands and feet, cutting off circulation. Symptoms are pallor and coldness of fingers and toes.

RECRUITMENT TEST A hearing test to compare loudness of a tone as perceived by each ear.

REFRACTION A test to determine need for corrective lenses for defective vision.

REGIMEN A set of rules to be followed for treating illness or sustaining health.

REGURGITATION The return of small amounts of food from the stomach. Also used to describe the blood flowing backward through incompletely closed heart valves.

REHABILITATION Restoration of functioning after disease or injury.

REJECTION PHENOMENON The tendency of the body to destroy tissues transplanted from another body.

RELAPSE A reversal of recovery from a disease or illness.

REMISSION Temporary abatement of symptoms of a disease.

RENAL FAILURE Failure of kidney functions.

RENAL HYPERTENSION High blood pressure resulting from kidney disease. See *HYPERTENSION.*

RENAL OSTEODYSTROPHY A childhood bone disease resulting from chronic renal (kidney) failure. Also *UREMIC BONE DISEASE.*

RENAL RICKETS A form of renal osteodystrophy in which the bone becomes porous and bends easily. See *RENAL OSTEODYSTROPHY.*

RESIDUAL Remaining effects of illness or injury as in "residual disability."

RESISTANCE Ability to withstand exposure to a disease.

RESPIRATORY DISTRESS SYNDROME A condition of newborn children, particularly prematurely born, which prevents babies from filling their lungs with air due to a lack of normal chemical mechanism which usually develops shortly before birth.

RESTLESS LEGS An involuntary movement of the legs while the subject lies down for a prolonged period.

RESUSCITATION Revival of persons apparently dead. Includes but not limited to cardiopulmonary respiration and artificial respiration. See *ARTIFICIAL RESPIRATION, CPR.*

RETICULOCYTE COUNT A blood test for anemia.

RETINITIS Inflammation of the retina of the eye. See *RETINOPATHY.*

RETINOBLASTOMA Cancer of the retina.

RETINOPATHY Disease of the retina of the eye. See *RETINITIS, RETINOBLASTOMA.*

RHEUMATIC FEVER A streptococcus infection causing joint inflammation and fever which subside, but the heart valves may be permanently damaged.

RHEUMATISM A general term for any painful disorder of the joints. Includes rheumatoid arthritis, osteoarthritis, gout and fibrosis.

RHEUMATOID ARTHRITIS A chronic disease of the fibrous connective tissue around a joint with a small painful nodule under the skin, especially at finger knuckles and wrists.

RHINITIS Inflammation of the lining of the nose.

RHINOPHYMA Growth of nodules in the nose.

RHONCHUS A wheeze when breathing.

RICKETS Malformation of bones due to lack of vitamin D.

RIGOR Violent shivering, usually at the start of a fever.

RINGWORM A fungus disease of the skin. Symptoms are itching, a red sore, which expands outward as a ring, while the center heals with a yellow scaly appearance. Related to athlete's foot. Also *TINEA*.

RINNE TEST A test of conductive hearing using a tuning fork.

ROCKY MOUNTAIN SPOTTED FEVER A bacterial disease transmitted by ticks. Symptoms are prostrating fever and a rash of red spots.

ROMBERG TEST A test of balance.

ROSACEA Red discoloration of the nose and sometimes the face. May be hereditary, often attributed to heavy drinking, but that is only one cause. Also known as drinker's nose.

ROSEOLA The pink rash of measles. See *MEASLES*.

ROUNDWORM An intestinal parasite, usually contracted from contact with dogs and cats.

RUBELLA See *GERMAN MEASLES*.

RUBELLA TEST A blood test to determine immunity against rubella (German measles).

RUBEOLA See *MEASLES*.

RUPTURE See *HERNIA*.

RUPTURED DISC Torn cartilage pad between vertebrae. May cause extreme pain by exerting pressure against the spinal cord.

S

SGOT (SERUM GLUTAMIC OXALACETIC TRANSAMINASE) TEST A blood test for liver disease.

SGPT (SERUM GLUTAMIC-PYRUVIC TRANSAMINASE) TEST A blood test for liver disease. May also indicate a heart disease.

SISI (SHORT INCREMENT SENSITIVITY INDEX) TEST A hearing test to determine ability to perceive changes in loudness.

SABIN VACCINE A live virus vaccine for poliomyelitis, administered by mouth.

ST. ANTHONY'S FIRE See *ERYSIPELAS*.

ST. VITUS' DANCE A disorder of children, usually resulting from rheumatic fever, characterized by uncontrolled, jerky movements. Mild cases often thought to be "fidgeting." It clears up in two to three months. Also *CHOREA MINOR, SYDENHAM'S CHOREA*.

SALK VACCINE A killed virus vaccine for poliomyelitis. Injected into a muscle.

SAN JOAQUIN VALLEY FEVER See *COCCIDIOSIS*.

SALMONELLA A bacterial infection of food which causes food poisoning.

SALPINGITIS An infection of the Fallopian tubes. Symptom is acute lower abdominal pain similar to appendicitis. Scarring could result in sterility.

SARCOMA Cancer of the connective tissue.

SCABIES A skin inflammation caused by a parasite, the mite. Usual sites are soft, moist skin: armpits or groin. Major symptom is itching; the condition is often called "the itch." Also *CUBAN ITCH, SEVEN-YEAR ITCH*.

SCARLATINA See *SCARLET FEVER*.

SCARLET FEVER A streptococcus infection which usually affects children. Spread by airborne droplets, or contaminated food and drink. Symptoms are fever, nausea, sore throat and flushed face. A spotty rash spreads over the body. Also *SCARLATINA*.

SCHICK TEST A test to determine susceptibility to diptheria. A small amount of diptheria toxin is injected under the skin. A red spot indicates susceptibility.

SCHIZOID PERSONALITY An individual who is withdrawn, over-sensitive and aloof. Sometimes becomes eccentric in behavior.

SCHIZOPHRENIA A psychosis in which the individual loses touch with reality, often involving delusions of grandeur and persecution, and hallucinations. Also *SPLIT PERSONALITY*.

SCHLATTER'S DISEASE Malformed growth of lower leg bone. See *OSTEOCHRONDROSIS*.

SCHWABACH TEST A hearing test involving a tuning fork held behind the ear.

SCIATICA Persistent pain in the leg caused by irritation of the sciatic nerve, usually from a ruptured disc. See *RUPTURED DISC*.

SCLERODERMA A skin condition associated with hard, yellow appearance, most often in women. Caused by glandular changes.

SCLEROSIS Thickening or hardening, as in arteriosclerosis (hardening of the arteries). Multiple sclerosis is thickening of connective tissue throughout the body.

SCOLIOSIS Sideways curvature of the spine.

SCOTOMA A blind spot in the eye.

SCRATCH TEST A skin test for allergies. Samples of suspected substances are introduced into scratches on the skin.

SCROFULA Tuberculosis of lymph glands in the neck with ulceration of the exterior skin.

SCURVY Vitamin C deficiency. Symptoms are bleeding

subcutaneously from the gums, into joints. Teeth become loose.

SEA SICKNESS See *MOTION SICKNESS*.

SEBACEOUS CYST Oily, fatty deposit under the skin from blockage of a sebaceous gland. Harmless. Also *WEN*.

SEBORRHEA Greasy skin from excessive activity of the sebaceous glands, often associated with acne or dandruff.

SEBORRHEIC DERMATITIS See *DANDRUFF*.

SECRETORY OTITIS Ear stuffiness with deafness and sometimes secretions. Also *CATARRH OF THE EAR, SEROUS OTITIS*.

SEDENTARY Insufficient physical activity.

SEISURE Sudden attack or convulsion.

SEMINOMA Cancer of the testicles.

SENESCENCE Aging of the body.

SENILITY Loss of mental ability and memory as the result of age-related deterioration of brain cells. Typical symptom is failure to remember recent events but having a clear memory of the distant past.

SEPSIS Infections which destroy tissue.

SEPTICEMIA See *BLOOD POISONING*.

SEPTIC SORE THROAT See *STREP THROAT*.

SERUM 1. The liquid part of the blood. 2. The serum from the blood of a person or animal which has built immunity to a specific disease.

SEVEN-YEAR ITCH See *SCABIES*.

SHAKING PALSY See *PARKINSON'S DISEASE*.

SHEEPHERDER'S DISEASE See *LEPTOSPIROSIS*.

SHINGLES See *HERPES ZOSTER*.

SHIATSU See *ACCUPRESSURE*.

SHOCK Sudden lowering of the blood pressure from injury or illness. The reduced circulation to the brain can be lethal. Raising the legs lets blood reach the brain.

SIBLING A sister or brother.

SICK HEADACHE A headache accompanied by nausea. Often confused with migraine headache. See *MIGRAINE HEADACHE*.

SICKLE CELL ANEMIA A hereditary defect of red blood cells, found primarily in negroes. Red cells are sickle (new moon) shaped and block capillaries, creating scar tissue and pain.

SICKLE CELL TRAIT Genetic condition in which sickle cell anemia gene is received by only one parent. The subject is a carrier but suffers problems only under unusual conditions. See *SICKLE CELL ANEMIA*.

SIDEROSIS Deposits of iron in the lung.

SIGMOIDOSCOPY Inspection of the rectum with a special instrument (sigmoidoscope) which has a light at the end of a viewing tube.

SILICOSIS Silica dust in the lungs.

SINUSITIS Inflammation or infection of the sinuses, which are cavities in the head connecting into the nose. Symptoms are stuffiness, headache and facial pain. Caused by colds, allergies, even damp weather.

SITZ BATH Sitting in a hot bath for relief of pain of rectum or vagina.

SKIN TESTS Tests for immunity or sensitivity, performed by placing various materials on the skin or under it to see if irritation results. See *PATCH TEST, SCRATCH TEST*.

SLEEPING SICKNESS An infectious disease originating in Africa. Transmitted by tsetse flies. Symptoms are lassitude and inability to stay awake for any length of time.

SLIPPED DISC See *RUPTURED DISC*.

SLIT LAMP See *BIOMICROSCOPE*.

SMALLPOX A highly infectious disease caused by a virus. Symptoms are a flu-like fever, backache, a spotty rash followed by pustules. There is usually permanent scarring. Also *VARIOLA*.

SMOKER'S PATCHES See *LEUKOPLAKIA*.

SNAKE BITE There are two types of snake venom: 1. poisons which affect the nerves and cause organ paralysis, and 2. poisons which destroy the structure of the blood. Alcohol makes the situation worse, regardless of the type of poison.

SNEEZE An explosive expulsion of air following tickling feeling in the nose. Also *STERNUTATION*.

SNORING A rasping noise produced during sleep.

SOLUBLE Capable of being disolved, usually in water.

SOLVENT A liquid which will disolve solid substances. Water, alcohol, oil and many chemicals are solvents.

SOMNAMBULISM Sleepwalking.

SONOGRAPHY Examination by high frequency sound waves. The instrument (sonograph) shows a detailed, multi-dimensional view of the organ or body area.

SPASM An involuntary, convulsive, muscular contraction.

SPASTIC PARALYSIS See *CEREBRAL PALSY*.

SPECIFIC GRAVITY A test of urine to measure wastes to evaluate kidney function.

SPECULUM An instrument to expand openings for examination. Used especially in vaginal examinations.

SPHINCTER A closing (valve) mechanism which works like a pursestring. The anus is a sphincter.

SPHYGMOMANOMETER A blood pressure instrument, utilizing a "cuff" around the arm and a gauge.

SPIDER FINGERS See *ARACHNODACTYLY*.

SPINA BIFIDA A congenital condition of incomplete vertebrae in the lower part of the spine. There may be numbness or paralysis and also faulty cerebrospinal fluid drainage.

SPINAL See *CAUDAL ANESTHETIC*.

SPINAL TAP See *LUMBAR PUNCTURE*.

SPLENOMEGALY Enlargement of the spleen.

SPONDYLITIS Inflammation of the spinal vertebrae.

See *ANKYLOSING SPONDYLITIS.*

SPONDYLOLISTHESIS A congenital condition of the spine with partial dislocation of a lumbar vertebra.

SPOTS BEFORE THE EYES See *MUSCAE VOLITANTES.*

SPRAIN Torn ligaments in a joint, with pain and swelling. Most commonly in an ankle or wrist.

SPRUE A nutritional deficiency with chronic diarrhea, anemia and weight loss.

SQUINT A deviating eye which turns in or out. See *ESOTROPIA, EXOTROPIA, STRABISMUS.*

STAMEY TEST A test of kidney function. Two catheters (tubes) are inserted through the urinary tract to collect the urine output of each kidney separately.

STAMMERING See *STUTTERING.*

STAPEDECTOMY An operation to replace the moving part (stapes) of the middle ear with a plastic substitute to restore hearing.

STAPHLOCOCCUS A common germ found on the skin and in the ground which causes infections with inflammation and pus.

STARVATION Extreme malnutrition.

STENOSIS A narrowing of a canal; a stricture, particularly of a heart valve.

STERILITY Inability to reproduce. May occur in either male or female.

STERILIZATION Operation to make a person sterile. See *TUBAL LIGATION, VASECTOMY.*

STERNUTATION See *SNEEZE.*

STETHOSCOPE An instrument for detecting sounds in the chest and other body areas. Most commonly recognized doctor's instrument, with two tubes leading to the doctor's ears. Invented in 1816.

STIFF NECK 1. Pain from muscular strain. 2. Pain from arthritis. 3. Congenital, painless uneveness of the muscles at the sides of the neck. Also *TORTICOLLIS.*

STILL BIRTH A baby dead at birth.

STILL'S DISEASE A form of juvenile rheumatoid arthritis which affects the entire system. See *JUVENILE RHEUMATOID ARTHRITIS.*

STITCH A pain in the abdomen upon rigorous exercise like jogging.

STIMULANT A drug which increases mental and/or bodily acivity.

STOKES-ADAMS ATTACK A heart block causing unconsciousness.

STOMACH NOISES See *BORBORYGMUS.*

STOMATITIS Inflammation of the mucous membrane of the mouth. See *APHTHOUS STOMATITIS, VINCENT'S DISEASE.*

STOOPED SHOULDERS See *KYPHOSIS.*

STRABISMUS Eyes do not point in the same direction. See *ESOPHORIA, ESOTROPIA, EXOPHORIA, EXOTROPIA, SQUINT.*

STRAIN An injury to a muscle caused by excessive stretching which may produce small tears in the tissue.

STRANGULATION Cutting off blood circulation to part of the body. Especially in hernia where a loop of intestine has been pinched.

STRANGURY Difficulty in urninating, usually painful.

STRAWBERRY MARK See *BIRTHMARK.*

STREP THROAT Streptococcus infection of the throat. Also *SEPTIC SORE THROAT.*

STREPTOCOCCUS A bacteria associated with severe infections such as strep throat and rheumatic fever. See *RHEUMATIC FEVER, STREP THROAT.*

STRESS Anything which interferes with physical or mental functioning. Used especially for emotional pressures.

STRESS TEST An electrocardiogram taken while the subject is exercising on a treadmill, a bicycle or set of 12-inch steps.

STROKE Impairment of circulation to the brain which might result in unconsciousness, and death of brain tissue causing paralysis, loss of memory. See *APOPLEXY.*

STUTTERING Difficulty in speech marked by spasmodic repetition of certain sounds. Also *STAMMERING.*

STYE See *HORDEOLUM.*

SUBCUTANEOUS Beneath the skin.

SUBDURAL HEMATOMA A bruise or collection of blood below the skin. See *BRUISE.*

SUBLUXATION Partial dislocation.

SUDAMEN See *PRICKLY HEAT.*

SUGAR DIABETES See *DIABETES.*

SUNBURN Overexposure to the sun causing skin symptoms similar to burning. First degree involves only the top layer of skin. Second degree affects two layers and the third degree (highly dangerous) involves all three skin layers with possible damage to underlying tissue.

SUNSTROKE See *HEATSTROKE.*

SUPPOSITORY A medication in solid stick or cone form which, when inserted into a body opening (vagina or rectum), disolves into a liquid with the heat of the body.

SUPPURATION Formation of pus.

SUTURE A tie (thread stitch) used to close a wound or operation.

SWAYBACK See *LORDOSIS.*

SWEATING Excretion of water and salt from sweat glands as a cooling mechanism to regulate body temperatures. Also *PERSPIRATION.*

SYCOSIS BARBAE See *BARBER'S ITCH.*

SYDENHAM'S CHOREA Also *CHOREA MINOR.* See *ST. VITUS' DANCE.*

SYMPATHECTOMY An operation to sever sympathetic nerves to prevent spasm of blood vessels.

SYMPTOM A manifestation of a disease.

SYNCOPE See *FAINTING.*

SYNDROME A particular pattern of symptoms.

SYNOVITIS Inflammation of the membranes which line the joints.

SYPHILIS An infectious viral venereal disease. Initial symptom is a chancre, a hard lump which usually ulcerates. Lymph glands in the groin may also swell.

T

TAB (TYPHOID, PARATYPHOID A & B) VACCINE A combination vaccine for typhoid and typhoid like diseases.

TNS (TRANSCUTANEOUS NERVE STIMULATION) An electric generator that blocks nerve transmission of pain by sending minute electrical charges into the area.

TABES A condition marked by difficulty in walking, a secondary effect of syphilis. Also *LOCOMOTOR ATAXIA*.

TACHYCARDIA Unusually rapid heart beat. See *ARRHYTHMIA*.

TACHYPHAGIA Rapid eating.

TAENIA See *TAPEWORM*.

TALIPES See *CLUBFOOT*.

TANTRUM A fit of bad temper, a violent, uncontrolled display of rage. Also *TEMPER TANTRUM*.

TAPEWORM A parasitic worm shaped like a tape (flat in crosssection) infesting human intestines. Also *TAENIA*.

TAY-SACHS DISEASE A hereditary disease restricted to Jews of Eastern European ancestry. The child receives two defective genes from its parents and suffers degenerative brain damage which results in death by the fourth year. May be detected before birth by use of amniocentesis. See *AMNIOCENTESIS*.

TEMPERATURE Normal temperature range for most people is 97° to 99° Fahrenheit (36° to 37.2° Celsius), measured in the mouth, but varies from one degree or more lower in early morning to one degree or more higher in the evening. Prolonged temperatures over 105°F. can be damaging.

TEMPER TANTRUM See *TANTRUM*.

TENDONITIS Inflammation of tendons.

TENNIS ELBOW Painful muscles below the elbow, caused by minor tears in the tissues. Generally results from playing tennis or squash.

TERATOMA A tumor which mimics other tissue.

TESTICLES, UNDESCENDED Testicles originate in the lower groin but descend into the scrotum. In some children, one or both testicles do not descend. Hormones are produced, but the sperm produced are not viable.

TETANUS A bacterial disease often contracted from soil or dirty objects which penetrate the flesh. Toxins produced by the bacteria cause spasm of the jaw muscles, and later other muscles including those responsible for breathing. Also *LOCKJAW*.

TETANUS IMMUNEGLOBULIN Immunication for tetanus.

TETANY Muscle twitching and sustained contraction (cramps). Often caused by low levels of calcium in the blood.

THERMOGRAPHY An infrared image on photographic film of tumors of the breast.

THERMOMETER An instrument to measure temperature in the mouth or anus. Available as glass tubes containing mercury, or as an electronic instrument with a digital readout.

THORACENTESIS Draining fluid from around the lung by inserting a needle through the chest wall.

THORACOTOMY An operation to open the thorax (chest).

THROMBOANGILITIS OBILITERANS See *BUERGER'S DISEASE*.

THROMBOPHLEBITIS Inflammation of a vein obstructed by clotted blood. Also *PHLEBITIS*.

THROMBOSIS Formation of a clot which blocks circulation in an artery or vein.

THROMBUS A clot. See *THROMBOPHLEBITIS*.

THRUSH A fungus infection of the mouth.

THYROIDITIS Inflammation of the thyroid gland.

TIC A reflex action, such as a blink, head bobbing, cough, repeated in spasmodic fashion.

TIC DOULOUREUX See *TRIGEMINAL NEURALGIA*.

TICK Spiderlike insect which attaches itself to skin of animals and man. May transmit typhus and Rocky Mountain Spotted Fever.

TINEA See *RINGWORM*.

TINEA CRURIS See *JOCK ITCH*.

TIN EAR See *CAULIFLOWER EAR*.

TINNITUS Spontaneous sounds in the ear: ringing, buzzing or hissing. May be caused by drugs, Meniere's disease, inflammation and blockage of the eustachian tube, or no known cause.

TOLERANCE Gradually increasing resistance to the effects of a drug or medicine.

TONE DECAY TEST A hearing test to determine how well the ears can conduct a tone without fatigue.

TONOMETRY An examination of the eye for glaucoma. An instrument (tonometer) is placed against the eyeball and measures the internal pressure. See *GLAUCOMA*.

TONSILITIS Infection or inflammation of the tonsils. See *QUINSY*.

TOPHUS Uric acid deposit in the tissues, particularly in the ear, a result of untreated gout. See *GOUT*.

TORTICOLLIS Spasm of the neck muscles which pulls the head to one side. In infants usually the result of a birth injury. Also *WRY NECK*.

TOTAL CHOLESTEROL TEST A test for the level of cholesterol in the blood. Normal range is 140 to 265 milligrams per 100 milliliters (mg/100 ml).

TOTAL PROTEIN TEST A blood test for protein levels indicating metabolic function. Normal range is 6 to 8.5 grams per 100 milliliters (g/100 ml).

TOURNIQUET A binding which slows circulation in a limb, used to prevent excessive blood loss or the spread of snake or insect venom.

TOXEMIA See *BLOOD POISONING*.

TOXOPLASMOSIS Infection by protozoa (small, single cell animals), usually harmless, but may damage unborn child if contracted by the pregnant mother.

TRACHEITIS Inflammation of the trachea (windpipe).

TRACHOMA An infection of the inner lining of the eyelids and the conjunctiva (covering of the front of the eye). Also *PINK EYE*.

TRAUMA A wound or any damage to the body.

TREMOR The shaking of a part of the body. Also *PALSY*.

TRENCH MOUTH See *VINCENT'S ANGINA, VINCENT'S DISEASE*.

TRICHINOSIS A parasitic disease endemic in pigs and transmitted to man by eating undercooked pork. Symptoms are fever and pain, which may become chronic as the tiny worms embed themselves in the muscles and various organs.

TRICHOMONIASIS See *TRICHOMONUS*.

TRICHOMONUS A bacterial infection of the vagina. Symptoms are irritation and discharge. May also infect men by contact. Also *TRICHOMONIASIS*.

TRICK KNEE See *FOOTBALL KNEE*.

TRIFOCAL A spectacle lens with three focusing distances — one for near, one for middle distance, one for distant vision.

TRIGEMINAL NEURALGIA A severe pain on one side of the face which occurs intermittantly, usually in older persons. Often caused by exposure to cold. Also *TIC DOULOUREUX*.

TRIGLYCERIDES TEST A blood test for levels of fat in the blood. Normal range is 50 to 170 milligrams per 100 milliliters (mg/100 ml).

TRISMUS Spasm of the jaw muscles. See *TETANUS*.

TROPIA A deviated eye. See *ESOTROPIA, EXOTROPIA*.

TUBAL LIGATION Tying off surgically or cutting the Fallopian tubes to sterilize a woman.

TUBERCULOSIS A bacterial disease which most commonly affects the lungs, but may also infect joints, organs and the skin. Also *CONSUMPTION*.

TUBULAR PREGNANCY Pregnancy in a Fallopian tube. See *ECTOPIC PREGNANCY*.

TULAREMIA A bacterial disease related to bubonic plague affecting rabbits. Also *RABBIT FEVER*.

TUMOR A swelling, usually composed of tissue growth (neoplasm). Benign tumors are harmless, malignant tumors are cancerous.

TUNNEL VISION The inability to use the full field of vision. See *GLAUCOMA*.

TYPHOID FEVER A bacterial disease usually spread by contaminated food or drink. Some poeple can harbor it without symptoms (a carrier). Symptoms are fever and occasionally a rash and various aches and pains. Also *ENTERIC FEVER*.

TYPHUS A bacterial disease, usually transmitted by lice. Symptoms are a prostrating fever, rash and occasionally pneumonia.

U

URI (UPPER RESPIRATORY INFECTION) See *COMMON COLD*.

ULCER An open sore other than a wound. An ulcer may fail to heal because of poor circulation, continued injury, irritation or infection. See *PEPTIC ULCER*.

ULTRASONOGRAPHY An ultrasound test to determine cysts, blood clots and tumors in the eye. See *ULTRASOUND*.

UNCONSCIOUSNESS See *COMA*.

UNDULANT FEVER See *BRUCELLOSIS*.

UPPER GI SERIES An X-ray examination of the upper gastro-intestinal (digestive) tract. A radiopaque solution (barium sulfate) is swallowed by the subject.

UREMIA Elevated urea levels in the blood, caused by kidney malfunction.

UREMIC BONE DISEASE See *RENAL OSTEODYSTROPHY*.

URETHRITIS Inflammation of the urethra, the outlet from the bladder.

URIC ACID TEST A blood test for gout. Normal range for males is 2.5 to 8.5 milligrams per 100 milliliters (mg/100 ml); for females 2.5 to 6.5 milligrams.

URINALYSIS Examination of urine for disease.

UROGRAPHY X-ray examinations of the urinary system.

URTICARIA See *HIVES*.

UVEITIS Inflammation of the uveal tract: the iris of the eye and the membrane behind the retina.

V

VDRL (VENERAL DISEASE RESEARCH LABORATORY) TEST A blood test for syphilis, often done as a premarital examination.

VACCINATION Innoculation against disease by injecting an anti-toxin or a vaccine.

VAGINITIS An infection or inflammation of the vagina.

VARCICELLA See *CHICKENPOX*.

VARICOCELE Varicosity of the veins of a testicle, usually on the left side.

VARICOSE VEINS Swollen and malformed veins, especially of the legs.

VARIOLA See *SMALLPOX*.

VASCULITIS Inflammation of the blood vessels.

VASECTOMY A simple operation to sterilize a male.

The vas deferens which carries sperm from the testicles to the prostate) is cut or tied off.

VECTORCARDIOGRAPHY Three-dimensional electrocardiogram of the heart. See *EKG*.

VENEREAL DISEASE Disease transmitted through sexual intercourse. See *GONORRHEA, HERPES SIMPLEX II, SYPHILIS.*

VENOGRAPHY An examination by injecting radiopaque solution into a vein and taking X-rays.

VENTRICULITIS Inflammation of the ventricles of the heart.

VENTRICULOGRAPHY An X-ray test to determine blood clots, tumors, abscesses, etc., in the brain. Air is injected through holes drilled in the skull.

VERTIGO Dizziness; giddiness, a feeling that surroundings are revolving around the subject. Also *DIZZINESS.*

VESICLE Blister.

VINCENT'S ANGINA Also *TRENCH MOUTH, VINCENT'S DISEASE.*

VINCENT'S DISEASE Also *TRENCH MOUTH, VINCENT'S ANGINA.*

VIRAL GASTROENTERITIS Also *STOMACH FLU.* See *INTESTINAL FLU.*

VIRAL URI See *COMMON COLD, URI.*

VISUAL FIELDS A test to determine the area viewed by each eye.

VITILIGO White patches of skin due to loss of pigment. Harmless, but cause not known.

VOLVULUS Twisting of a loop of intestine to abstruct food passage.

VOMITING A reflex action in which stomach contents are explosively ejected through the esophagus and mouth.

W

WBC (WHITE BLOOD CELL) COUNT A blood test. Microscopic count of white blood cells.

WALL EYES One eye turns outward. See *EXOTROPIA, SQUINT, STRABISMUS.*

WART Small tumor of the skin caused by a virus. A rough, callous-like lump, often found in clumps.

WASSERMAN TEST A blood test for syphilis.

WATER ON THE BRAIN See *HYDROCEPHALUS.*

WATER ON THE KNEE Collection of lymphatic fluid in the knee joint, usually caused by injury.

WATER PILL See *DIURETIC.*

WEBER TEST A test of conductive hearing using a tuning fork.

WEN See *SEBACEOUS CYST.*

THE WHITES See *LEUKORREA.*

WHOOPING COUGH A bacterial disease of childhood. Extremely infectious with violent, uncontrollable bursts of coughing, the main symptom, often accompanied by vomiting. Also *PERTUSSIS.*

WILMS' TUMOR A disease of infants in which a kidney becomes cancerous with few symptoms except for distention of the abdomen. Also *NEPHROBLASTOMA.*

WOOL SORTER'S DISEASE See *ANTHRAX.*

WOUND There are five types of injuries to the body (wounds): abrasion (scrape), contusion (bruise), incision (cut), laceration (tear), and puncture.

WRY NECK See *TORTICOLLIS.*

X

X-RAY A photographic device which uses radiation to expose photographic film. The radiation used penetrates soft tissues, leaving images of bones and some growths.

XANTHELASMA Small yellow nodules under the skin of the eyelids in older people who have a high level of blood lipids (fats).

XANTHOMA Deposits of fatty substances in the skin. Usually confined to the eyelids. See *XANTHELASMA.*

XERODERMA Abnormal skin dryness. Also *ICHTHYOSIS.*

XEROGRAPHY See *MAMMOGRAPHY.*

XEROMAMMOGRAPHY An X-ray examination of the breast which produces a blue and white photographic print instead of a negative. See *MAMMOGRAPHY.*

XEROPHTHALMIA Dryness of the cornea, sometimes accompanied by opacity.

XEROSIS Abnormal dryness of the eye. Lack of tears. See *XEROPHTHALMIA.*

Y

YELLOW FEVER A virus infection transmitted by mosquitoes. Symptoms are violent fever with jaundice from liver inflammation. Kidneys and heart are also affected.

Z

ZOONOSIS Any animal disease which affects man.

MOTHER

Name _____

Date of Birth _____ Blood Type _____ Rh Factor _____

Immunizations	Date	Immunizations	Date	Immunizations	Date
Polio, type ____	_____	15 years	_____	50 years	_____
DPT	_____	DT booster	_____	Tetanus booster	_____
Rubella	_____	20 years	_____	55 years	_____
Measles	_____	Tetanus booster	_____	DT booster	_____
Mumps	_____	25 years	_____	60 years	_____
M/M/R	_____	DT booster	_____	Tetanus booster	_____
Smallpox	_____	30 years	_____	Influenza	_____
Other (list)	_____	Tetanus booster	_____	Influenza	_____
_____	_____	35 years	_____	Influenza	_____
_____	_____	DT booster	_____	Influenza	_____
_____	_____	40 years	_____	Influenza	_____
_____	_____	Tetanus booster	_____	Influenza	_____
_____	_____	45 years	_____	Influenza	_____
		DT booster	_____	Influenza	_____

IMMUNIZATION – DEFINITIONS

Polio - Sabin oral type (OPV)

     - Salk injected type (IPV)

DPT - Diptheria/Pertussis/Tetanus

     Pertussis - Whooping Cough

     Tetanus - Lockjaw

DT - Diptheria/Tetanus

M/M/R - Measles/Mumps/Rubella

Rubella - German (3-day) Measles

Physical Condition (birth defects, limitations from injury or disease)

_____

_____

_____

ALLERGIES:

To medicines (list): _____

To foods (list): _____

To chemicals or cleansers (list): _____

To substances (Hay Fever): _____

Other (list): _____

VISION:

	At Age 3 Years	At Age 6 Years
Left Eye (OS)		
Near Sighted (myopia)	☐	☐
Far Sighted (hyperopia)	☐	☐

	At Age 3 Years	At Age 6 Years
Right Eye (OD)		
Near Sighted (myopia)	☐	☐
Far Sighted (hyperopia)	☐	☐

LEFT EYE

Check
- ☐ Astigmatism
- ☐ Crossed eyes (strabismus)
- ☐ Prism
- ☐ Other (list): _____

_____

_____

_____

RIGHT EYE

Check
- ☐ Astigmatism
- ☐ Crossed eyes (strabismus)
- ☐ Prism
- ☐ Other (list): _____

_____

_____

_____

REFRACTION (Transfer from Eye Doctor's Prescription)

Date	Eye	Sphere	Cylinder	Axis	Prism
	OS				
	OD				
Add for near:			Add for intermediate:		

Date	Eye	Sphere	Cylinder	Axis	Prism
	OS				
	OD				
Add for near:			Add for intermediate:		

Date	Eye	Sphere	Cylinder	Axis	Prism
	OS				
	OD				
Add for near:			Add for intermediate:		

Date	Eye	Sphere	Cylinder	Axis	Prism
	OS				
	OD				
Add for near:			Add for intermediate:		

Date	Eye	Sphere	Cylinder	Axis	Prism
	OS				
	OD				
Add for near:			Add for intermediate:		

HEARING

Left Ear	Condition	Right Ear	Condition
At age 18 months	_____	At age 18 months	_____
At age 5 years	_____	At age 5 years	_____
Date: _____	_____	Date: _____	_____
Date: _____	_____	Date: _____	_____
Date: _____	_____	Date: _____	_____
Date: _____	_____	Date: _____	_____

CHILDHOOD DISEASES

Condition	Date	Complications
Chickenpox	_____	_____
German Measles (Rubella)	_____	_____
Infectious Mononucleosis	_____	_____
Measles (Rubeola)	_____	_____
Meningitis	_____	_____
Rheumatic Fever	_____	_____
Roseola	_____	_____
Scarlet Fever	_____	_____
Strep Throat	_____	_____
Other (list) _____	_____	_____
_____	_____	_____
_____	_____	_____
_____	_____	_____
_____	_____	_____
_____	_____	_____
_____	_____	_____
_____	_____	_____

LABORATORY TESTS

Have any of these procedures produced a *not* normal result? If so, please note below:

Test	Date	Doctor	Result	Treatment
Blood				
Complete Blood Count (CBC)				
Hemoglobin				
Hematocrit				
White Blood Count (WBC)				
Differential				
Red Blood Count				
Sedimentation Rate				
Blood Chemistry				
Glucose				
Triglicerides				
Cholesterol				
Uric Acid				
Other (list)				
Urinalysis				
Albumin				
Glucose				
White Blood Corpuscles				
Red Blood Corpuscles				
Specific Gravity				
Other (list)				

EKG				
X-Rays (list)				
PAP				
Tuberculin Test				
Other (list)				

MEDICAL RECORD

Date	Doctor	Diagnosis	Treatment	Residual Complications

RECORD OF PREGNANCIES

Name of child _____ Sex _____ Term _____months

Date of Delivery _____ Complications _____

Location of Delivery _____ City _____ State _____

Anesthetic and/or surgery used _____

Medications taken during pregnancy _____

_____

Illnesses during pregnancy _____

Name of child _____ Sex _____ Term _____months

Date of Delivery _____ Complications _____

Location of Delivery _____ City _____ State _____

Anesthetic and/or surgery used _____

Medications taken during pregnancy _____

_____

Illnesses during pregnancy _____

Name of child _____ Sex _____ Term _____months

Date of Delivery _____ Complications _____

Location of Delivery _____ City _____ State _____

Anesthetic and/or surgery used _____

Medications taken during pregnancy _____

_____

Illnesses during pregnancy _____

Name of child _____ Sex _____ Term _____months

Date of Delivery _____ Complications _____

Location of Delivery _____ City _____ State _____

Anesthetic and/or surgery used _____

Medications taken during pregnancy _____

_____

Illnesses during pregnancy _____

Name of child _____ Sex _____ Term _____months

Date of Delivery _____ Complications _____

Location of Delivery _____ City _____ State _____

Anesthetic and/or surgery used _____

Medications taken during pregnancy _____

_____

Illnesses during pregnancy _____

Name of child _____ Sex _____ Term _____months

Date of Delivery _____ Complications _____

Location of Delivery _____ City _____ State _____

Anesthetic and/or surgery used _____

Medications taken during pregnancy _____

_____

Illnesses during pregnancy _____

Name of child _____ Sex _____ Term _____months

Date of Delivery _____ Complications _____

Location of Delivery _____ City _____ State _____

Anesthetic and/or surgery used _____

Medications taken during pregnancy _____

_____

Illnesses during pregnancy _____

Name of child _____ Sex _____ Term _____months

Date of Delivery _____ Complications _____

Location of Delivery _____ City _____ State _____

Anesthetic and/or surgery used _____

Medications taken during pregnancy _____

_____

Illnesses during pregnancy _____

PRESCRIPTION DRUG RECORD

Date	Drug	Doctor	Result	Adverse Reaction or Allergy

PRESCRIPTION DRUG RECORD

Date	Drug	Doctor	Result	Adverse Reaction or Allergy

ENVIRONMENTAL EXPOSURE (Radiation, chemicals, toxic wastes, etc.)

Date Exposed	Where	How Long?	Type of Substance, Radiation or Condition	Treated By

ADULT TEETH

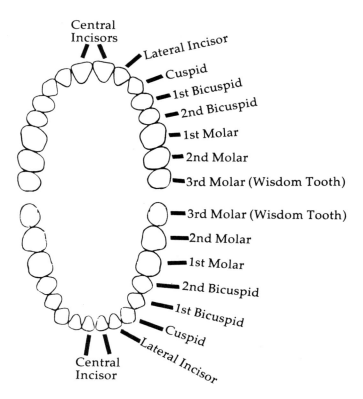

Central Incisors

Lateral Incisor

Cuspid

1st Bicuspid

2nd Bicuspid

1st Molar

2nd Molar

3rd Molar (Wisdom Tooth)

3rd Molar (Wisdom Tooth)

2nd Molar

1st Molar

2nd Bicuspid

1st Bicuspid

Cuspid

Lateral Incisor

Central Incisor

DENTAL RECORD

Date	Age	Treatment	Date	Age	Treatment

FATHER

Name _____

Date of Birth _____   Blood Type _____   Rh Factor _____

Immunizations	Date	Immunizations	Date	Immunizations	Date
Polio, type ___		15 years		50 years	
DPT		DT booster		Tetanus booster	
Rubella		20 years		55 years	
Measles		Tetanus booster		DT booster	
Mumps		25 years		60 years	
M/M/R		DT booster		Tetanus booster	
Smallpox		30 years		Influenza	
Other (list)		Tetanus booster		Influenza	
_____		35 years		Influenza	
_____		DT booster		Influenza	
_____		40 years		Influenza	
_____		Tetanus booster		Influenza	
_____		45 years		Influenza	
_____		DT booster		Influenza	

76

IMMUNIZATION – DEFINITIONS

Polio - Sabin oral type (OPV)   DT - Diptheria/Tetanus

       - Salk injected type (IPV)   M/M/R - Measles/Mumps/Rubella

DPT - Diptheria/Pertussis/Tetanus   Rubella - German (3-day) Measles

       Pertussis - Whooping Cough

       Tetanus - Lockjaw

Physical Condition (birth defects, limitations from injury or disease)

_____

_____

_____

ALLERGIES:

To medicines (list): _____

To foods (list): _____

To chemicals or cleansers (list): _____

To substances (Hay Fever): _____

Other (list): _____

VISION:

	At Age 3 Years	At Age 6 Years		At Age 3 Years	At Age 6 Years
Left Eye (OS)			Right Eye (OD)		
Near Sighted (myopia)	☐	☐	Near Sighted (myopia)	☐	☐
Far Sighted (hyperopia)	☐	☐	Far Sighted (hyperopia)	☐	☐

77

LEFT EYE

Check

☐ Astigmatism
☐ Crossed eyes (strabismus)
☐ Prism
☐ Other (list): _____

_____
_____
_____

RIGHT EYE

Check

☐ Astigmatism
☐ Crossed eyes (strabismus)
☐ Prism
☐ Other (list): _____

_____
_____
_____

REFRACTION (Transfer from Eye Doctor's Prescription)

Left

Date	Eye	Sphere	Cylinder	Axis	Prism
	OS				
	OD				
Add for intermediate:					
Add for near:					
Date	Eye	Sphere	Cylinder	Axis	Prism
	OS				
	OD				
Add for intermediate:					
Add for near:					
Date	Eye	Sphere	Cylinder	Axis	Prism
	OS				
	OD				
Add for intermediate:					
Add for near:					
Date	Eye	Sphere	Cylinder	Axis	Prism
	OS				
	OD				
Add for intermediate:					
Add for near:					
Date	Eye	Sphere	Cylinder	Axis	Prism
	OS				
	OD				
Add for intermediate:					
Add for near:					

Right

Date	Eye	Sphere	Cylinder	Axis	Prism
	OS				
	OD				
Add for intermediate:					
Add for near:					
Date	Eye	Sphere	Cylinder	Axis	Prism
	OS				
	OD				
Add for intermediate:					
Add for near:					
Date	Eye	Sphere	Cylinder	Axis	Prism
	OS				
	OD				
Add for intermediate:					
Add for near:					
Date	Eye	Sphere	Cylinder	Axis	Prism
	OS				
	OD				
Add for intermediate:					
Add for near:					
Date	Eye	Sphere	Cylinder	Axis	Prism
	OS				
	OD				
Add for intermediate:					
Add for near:					

HEARING

Left Ear	Condition	Right Ear	Condition
At age 18 months	_____	At age 18 months	_____
At age 5 years	_____	At age 5 years	_____
Date: _____	_____	Date: _____	_____
Date: _____	_____	Date: _____	_____
Date: _____	_____	Date: _____	_____
Date: _____	_____	Date: _____	_____

CHILDHOOD DISEASES

Condition	Date	Complications
Chickenpox	_____	_____
German Measles (Rubella)	_____	_____
Infectious Mononucleosis	_____	_____
Measles (Rubeola)	_____	_____
Meningitis	_____	_____
Rheumatic Fever	_____	_____
Roseola	_____	_____
Scarlet Fever	_____	_____
Strep Throat	_____	_____
Other (list) _____	_____	_____
_____	_____	_____
_____	_____	_____
_____	_____	_____
_____	_____	_____
_____	_____	_____
_____	_____	_____
_____	_____	_____

LABORATORY TESTS

Have any of these procedures produced a *not* normal result? If so, please note below:

Test	Date	Doctor	Result	Treatment
Blood				
Complete Blood Count (CBC)				
Hemoglobin				
Hematocrit				
White Blood Count (WBC)				
Differential				
Red Blood Count				
Sedimentation Rate				
Blood Chemistry				
Glucose				
Triglicerides				
Cholesterol				
Uric Acid				
Other (list)				
Urinalysis				
Albumin				
Glucose				
White Blood Corpuscles				
Red Blood Corpuscles				
Specific Gravity				
Other (list)				

EKG				
X-Rays (list)				
Prostatic Acid Phosphatase Test				
Tuberculin Test				
Other (list)				

MEDICAL RECORD

Date	Doctor	Diagnosis	Treatment	Residual Complications

PRESCRIPTION DRUG RECORD

Date	Drug	Doctor	Result	Adverse Reaction or Allergy

PRESCRIPTION DRUG RECORD

Date	Drug	Doctor	Result	Adverse Reaction or Allergy

ADULT TEETH

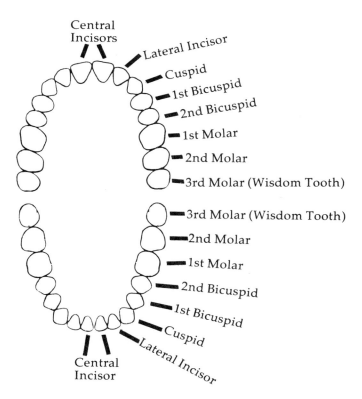

DENTAL RECORD

Date	Age	Treatment

Date	Age	Treatment

CHILD 1

Name _____

Date of Birth _____ Weight at Birth _____ Length at Birth _____ Blood Type _____ Rh Factor _____

Mother's health during pregnancy _____

Delivery complications _____

Place of Birth: Hospital _____ City _____ State _____ Birth Record Filed: _____

Condition of child at birth _____

Type of feeding _____ Age on solid foods _____ Age walking _____ Age talking _____

Immunizations	Date	Immunizations	Date	Immunizations	Date
Two months		12-15 months		10 years	
Polio, Type _____		Measles or M/M/R		Rubella	
DPT #1		18 Months		Tetanus booster	
Four months		Polio booster		15 years	
Polio, Type _____		DPT booster		DT booster	
DPT #2		Five years		20 years	
Six months		Polio booster		Tetanus booster	
Polio, Type _____		DT booster			
DPT #3					

86

IMMUNIZATION – DEFINITIONS

Polio - Sabin oral type (OPV)   DT - Diptheria/Tetanus

- Salk injected type (IPV)   M/M/R - Measles/Mumps/Rubella

DPT - Diptheria/Pertussis/Tetanus   Rubella - German (3-day) Measles

Pertussis - Whooping Cough

Tetanus - Lockjaw

Physical Condition (birth defects, limitations from injury or disease)

_____

_____

_____

ALLERGIES:

To medicines (list): _____

To foods (list): _____

To chemicals or cleansers (list): _____

To substances (Hay Fever): _____

Other (list): _____

VISION:

	At Age 3 Years	At Age 6 Years		At Age 3 Years	At Age 6 Years
Left Eye (OS)			Right Eye (OD)		
Near Sighted (myopia)	☐	☐	Near Sighted (myopia)	☐	☐
Far Sighted (hyperopia)	☐	☐	Far Sighted (hyperopia)	☐	☐

87

RIGHT EYE

Check

- [ ] Astigmatism
- [ ] Crossed eyes (strabismus)
- [ ] Prism
- [ ] Other (list): _____

_____
_____
_____

Date	Eye	Sphere	Cylinder	Axis	Prism
	OS				
	OD				
Add for near:					
			Add for intermediate:		
Date	OS				
	OD				
Add for near:					
			Add for intermediate:		
Date	OS				
	OD				
Add for near:					
			Add for intermediate:		
Date	OS				
	OD				
Add for near:					
			Add for intermediate:		
Date	OS				
	OD				
Add for near:					
			Add for intermediate:		

LEFT EYE

Check

- [ ] Astigmatism
- [ ] Crossed eyes (strabismus)
- [ ] Prism
- [ ] Other (list): _____

_____
_____
_____

REFRACTION (Transfer from Eye Doctor's Prescription)

Date	Eye	Sphere	Cylinder	Axis	Prism
	OS				
	OD				
Add for near:					
			Add for intermediate:		
Date	OS				
	OD				
Add for near:					
			Add for intermediate:		
Date	OS				
	OD				
Add for near:					
			Add for intermediate:		
Date	OS				
	OD				
Add for near:					
			Add for intermediate:		
Date	OS				
	OD				
Add for near:					
			Add for intermediate:		

LABORATORY TESTS

Have any of these procedures produced a *not* normal result? If so, please note below:

Test	Date	Doctor	Result	Treatment
Blood				
Complete Blood Count (CBC)				
Hemoglobin				
Hematocrit				
White Blood Count (WBC)				
Differential				
Red Blood Count				
Sedimentation Rate				
Blood Chemistry				
Glucose				
Triglicerides				
Cholesterol				
Uric Acid				
Other (list)				
Urinalysis				
Albumin				
Glucose				
White Blood Corpuscles				
Red Blood Corpuscles				
Specific Gravity				
Other (list)				

HEARING

Left Ear	Condition	Right Ear	Condition
At age 18 months	_____	At age 18 months	_____
At age 5 years	_____	At age 5 years	_____
Date: _____	_____	Date: _____	_____
Date: _____	_____	Date: _____	_____
Date: _____	_____	Date: _____	_____
Date: _____	_____	Date: _____	_____

CHILDHOOD DISEASES

Condition	Date	Complications
Chickenpox	_____	_____
German Measles (Rubella)	_____	_____
Infectious Mononucleosis	_____	_____
Measles (Rubeola)	_____	_____
Meningitis	_____	_____
Rheumatic Fever	_____	_____
Roseola	_____	_____
Scarlet Fever	_____	_____
Strep Throat	_____	_____
Other (list) _____	_____	_____
_____	_____	_____
_____	_____	_____
_____	_____	_____
_____	_____	_____
_____	_____	_____
_____	_____	_____
_____	_____	_____

EKG				
X-Rays (list)				
Tuberculin Test				
Other (list)				

MEDICAL RECORD

Date	Doctor	Diagnosis	Treatment	Residual Complications

PRESCRIPTION DRUG RECORD

Date	Drug	Doctor	Result	Adverse Reaction or Allergy

PRESCRIPTION DRUG RECORD

Date	Drug	Doctor	Result	Adverse Reaction or Allergy

BABY TEETH
(Ages Usually Lost)

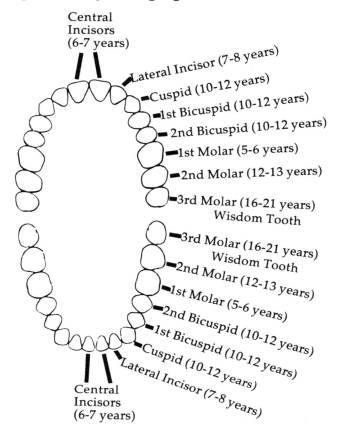

Central Incisors (6-7 years)

Lateral Incisor (7-8 years)
Cuspid (10-12 years)
1st Molar (9-11 years)
2nd Molar (9-11 years)

2nd Molar (9-11 years)
1st Molar (9-11 years)
Cuspid (10-12 years)
Lateral Incisor (7-8 years)

Central Incisors (6-7 years)

ADULT TEETH
(Ages Usually Emerging)

Central Incisors (6-7 years)

Lateral Incisor (7-8 years)
Cuspid (10-12 years)
1st Bicuspid (10-12 years)
2nd Bicuspid (10-12 years)
1st Molar (5-6 years)
2nd Molar (12-13 years)
3rd Molar (16-21 years) Wisdom Tooth

3rd Molar (16-21 years) Wisdom Tooth
2nd Molar (12-13 years)
1st Molar (5-6 years)
2nd Bicuspid (10-12 years)
1st Bicuspid (10-12 years)
Cuspid (10-12 years)
Lateral Incisor (7-8 years)

Central Incisors (6-7 years)

DENTAL RECORD

Date	Age	Treatment

Date	Age	Treatment

CHILD 2

Name _____

Date of Birth _____ Weight at Birth _____ Length at Birth _____ Blood Type _____ Rh Factor _____

Mother's health during pregnancy _____

Delivery complications _____

Place of Birth: Hospital _____ City _____ State _____ Birth Record Filed: _____

Condition of child at birth _____

Type of feeding _____ Age on solid foods _____ Age walking _____ Age talking _____

Immunizations	Date	Immunizations	Date	Immunizations	Date
Two months		12-15 months		10 years	
Polio, Type ___		Measles or M/M/R ___		Rubella ___	
DPT #1 ___		18 Months		Tetanus booster ___	
Four months		Polio booster ___		15 years	
Polio, Type ___		DPT booster ___		DT booster ___	
DPT #2 ___		Five years		20 years	
Six months		Polio booster ___		Tetanus booster ___	
Polio, Type ___		DT booster ___			
DPT #3 ___					

IMMUNIZATION – DEFINITIONS

Polio - Sabin oral type (OPV)

    - Salk injected type (IPV)

DPT - Diptheria/Pertussis/Tetanus

    Pertussis - Whooping Cough

    Tetanus - Lockjaw

DT - Diptheria/Tetanus

M/M/R - Measles/Mumps/Rubella

Rubella - German (3-day) Measles

Physical Condition (birth defects, limitations from injury or disease)

_____

_____

_____

ALLERGIES:

To medicines (list): _____

To foods (list): _____

To chemicals or cleansers (list): _____

To substances (Hay Fever): _____

Other (list): _____

VISION:

	At Age 3 Years	At Age 6 Years
Left Eye (OS)		
Near Sighted (myopia)	☐	☐
Far Sighted (hyperopia)	☐	☐

	At Age 3 Years	At Age 6 Years
Right Eye (OD)		
Near Sighted (myopia)	☐	☐
Far Sighted (hyperopia)	☐	☐

LEFT EYE

RIGHT EYE

Check

☐ Astigmatism

☐ Crossed eyes (strabismus)

☐ Prism

☐ Other (list): _____

_____

_____

_____

Check

☐ Astigmatism

☐ Crossed eyes (strabismus)

☐ Prism

☐ Other (list): _____

_____

_____

_____

REFRACTION (Transfer from Eye Doctor's Prescription)

Date	Eye	Sphere	Cylinder	Axis	Prism
	OS				
	OD				
Add for near:			Add for intermediate:		

Date	Eye	Sphere	Cylinder	Axis	Prism
	OS				
	OD				
Add for near:			Add for intermediate:		

Date	Eye	Sphere	Cylinder	Axis	Prism
	OS				
	OD				
Add for near:			Add for intermediate:		

Date	Eye	Sphere	Cylinder	Axis	Prism
	OS				
	OD				
Add for near:			Add for intermediate:		

Date	Eye	Sphere	Cylinder	Axis	Prism
	OS				
	OD				
Add for near:			Add for intermediate:		

LABORATORY TESTS

Have any of these procedures produced a *not* normal result? If so, please note below:

Test	Date	Doctor	Result	Treatment
Blood				
Complete Blood Count (CBC)				
Hemoglobin				
Hematocrit				
White Blood Count (WBC)				
Differential				
Red Blood Count				
Sedimentation Rate				
Blood Chemistry				
Glucose				
Triglicerides				
Cholesterol				
Uric Acid				
Other (list)				
Urinalysis				
Albumin				
Glucose				
White Blood Corpuscles				
Red Blood Corpuscles				
Specific Gravity				
Other (list)				

HEARING

Left Ear	Condition	Right Ear	Condition
At age 18 months	_____	At age 18 months	_____
At age 5 years	_____	At age 5 years	_____
Date: _____	_____	Date: _____	_____
Date: _____	_____	Date: _____	_____
Date: _____	_____	Date: _____	_____
Date: _____	_____	Date: _____	_____

CHILDHOOD DISEASES

Condition	Date	Complications
Chickenpox	_____	_____
German Measles (Rubella)	_____	_____
Infectious Mononucleosis	_____	_____
Measles (Rubeola)	_____	_____
Meningitis	_____	_____
Rheumatic Fever	_____	_____
Roseola	_____	_____
Scarlet Fever	_____	_____
Strep Throat	_____	_____
Other (list) _____	_____	_____
_____	_____	_____
_____	_____	_____
_____	_____	_____
_____	_____	_____
_____	_____	_____
_____	_____	_____
_____	_____	_____

EKG				
X-Rays (list)				
Tuberculin Test				
Other (list)				

MEDICAL RECORD

Date	Doctor	Diagnosis	Treatment	Residual Complications

PRESCRIPTION DRUG RECORD

Date	Drug	Doctor	Result	Adverse Reaction or Allergy

PRESCRIPTION DRUG RECORD

Date	Drug	Doctor	Result	Adverse Reaction or Allergy

BABY TEETH
(Ages Usually Lost)

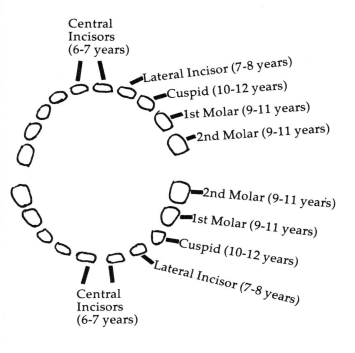

Central Incisors (6-7 years)

Lateral Incisor (7-8 years)
Cuspid (10-12 years)
1st Molar (9-11 years)
2nd Molar (9-11 years)

2nd Molar (9-11 years)
1st Molar (9-11 years)
Cuspid (10-12 years)
Lateral Incisor (7-8 years)

Central Incisors (6-7 years)

ADULT TEETH
(Ages Usually Emerging)

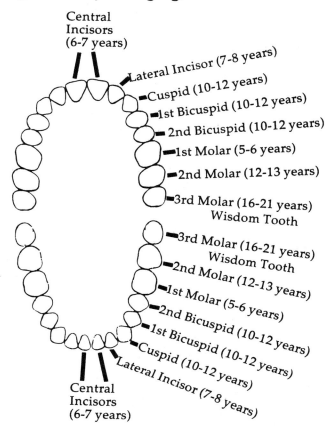

Central Incisors (6-7 years)

Lateral Incisor (7-8 years)
Cuspid (10-12 years)
1st Bicuspid (10-12 years)
2nd Bicuspid (10-12 years)
1st Molar (5-6 years)
2nd Molar (12-13 years)
3rd Molar (16-21 years) Wisdom Tooth

3rd Molar (16-21 years) Wisdom Tooth
2nd Molar (12-13 years)
1st Molar (5-6 years)
2nd Bicuspid (10-12 years)
1st Bicuspid (10-12 years)
Cuspid (10-12 years)
Lateral Incisor (7-8 years)

Central Incisors (6-7 years)

DENTAL RECORD

Date	Age	Treatment

Date	Age	Treatment

CHILD 3

Name _____

Date of Birth _____ Weight at Birth _____ Length at Birth _____ Blood Type _____ Rh Factor _____

Mother's health during pregnancy _____

Delivery complications _____

Place of Birth: Hospital _____ City _____ State _____ Birth Record Filed: _____

Condition of child at birth _____

Type of feeding _____ Age on solid foods _____ Age walking _____ Age talking _____

Immunizations	Date	Immunizations	Date	Immunizations	Date
Two months		12-15 months		10 years	
Polio, Type _____		Measles or M/M/R _____		Rubella _____	
DPT #1 _____		18 Months		Tetanus booster _____	
Four months		Polio booster _____		15 years	
Polio, Type _____		DPT booster _____		DT booster _____	
DPT #2 _____		Five years		20 years	
Six months		Polio booster _____		Tetanus booster _____	
Polio, Type _____		DT booster _____			
DPT #3 _____					

106

IMMUNIZATION – DEFINITIONS

Polio - Sabin oral type (OPV)   DT - Diptheria / Tetanus

     - Salk injected type (IPV)   M/M/R - Measles / Mumps / Rubella

DPT - Diptheria / Pertussis / Tetanus   Rubella - German (3-day) Measles

       Pertussis - Whooping Cough

       Tetanus - Lockjaw

Physical Condition (birth defects, limitations from injury or disease)

_____

_____

_____

ALLERGIES:

  To medicines (list): _____

  To foods (list): _____

  To chemicals or cleansers (list): _____

  To substances (Hay Fever): _____

  Other (list): _____

VISION:

	At Age 3 Years	At Age 6 Years
Left Eye (OS)		
Near Sighted (myopia)	☐	☐
Far Sighted (hyperopia)	☐	☐

	At Age 3 Years	At Age 6 Years
Right Eye (OD)		
Near Sighted (myopia)	☐	☐
Far Sighted (hyperopia)	☐	☐

107

RIGHT EYE

Check

- [ ] Astigmatism
- [ ] Crossed eyes (strabismus)
- [ ] Prism
- [ ] Other (list): _____

_____
_____

LEFT EYE

Check

- [ ] Astigmatism
- [ ] Crossed eyes (strabismus)
- [ ] Prism
- [ ] Other (list): _____

_____
_____

REFRACTION (Transfer from Eye Doctor's Prescription)

Date	Eye	Sphere	Cylinder	Axis	Prism
	OS				
	OD				
Add for near:			Add for intermediate:		

Date	Eye	Sphere	Cylinder	Axis	Prism
	OS				
	OD				
Add for near:			Add for intermediate:		

Date	Eye	Sphere	Cylinder	Axis	Prism
	OS				
	OD				
Add for near:			Add for intermediate:		

Date	Eye	Sphere	Cylinder	Axis	Prism
	OS				
	OD				
Add for near:			Add for intermediate:		

Date	Eye	Sphere	Cylinder	Axis	Prism
	OS				
	OD				
Add for near:			Add for intermediate:		

LABORATORY TESTS

Have any of these procedures produced a *not* normal result? If so, please note below:

Test	Date	Doctor	Result	Treatment
Blood				
Complete Blood Count (CBC)				
Hemoglobin				
Hematocrit				
White Blood Count (WBC)				
Differential				
Red Blood Count				
Sedimentation Rate				
Blood Chemistry				
Glucose				
Triglicerides				
Cholesterol				
Uric Acid				
Other (list)				
Urinalysis				
Albumin				
Glucose				
White Blood Corpuscles				
Red Blood Corpuscles				
Specific Gravity				
Other (list)				

HEARING

Left Ear	Condition	Right Ear	Condition
At age 18 months	_____	At age 18 months	_____
At age 5 years	_____	At age 5 years	_____
Date: _____	_____	Date: _____	_____
Date: _____	_____	Date: _____	_____
Date: _____	_____	Date: _____	_____
Date: _____	_____	Date: _____	_____

CHILDHOOD DISEASES

Condition	Date	Complications
Chickenpox	_____	_____
German Measles (Rubella)	_____	_____
Infectious Mononucleosis	_____	_____
Measles (Rubeola)	_____	_____
Meningitis	_____	_____
Rheumatic Fever	_____	_____
Roseola	_____	_____
Scarlet Fever	_____	_____
Strep Throat	_____	_____
Other (list) _____	_____	_____
_____	_____	_____
_____	_____	_____
_____	_____	_____
_____	_____	_____
_____	_____	_____
_____	_____	_____
_____	_____	_____

EKG				
X-Rays (list)				
Tuberculin Test				
Other (list)				

MEDICAL RECORD

Date	Doctor	Diagnosis	Treatment	Residual Complications

PRESCRIPTION DRUG RECORD

Date	Drug	Doctor	Result	Adverse Reaction or Allergy

PRESCRIPTION DRUG RECORD

Date	Drug	Doctor	Result	Adverse Reaction or Allergy

BABY TEETH
(Ages Usually Lost)

Central
Incisors
(6-7 years)

Lateral Incisor (7-8 years)

Cuspid (10-12 years)

1st Molar (9-11 years)

2nd Molar (9-11 years)

2nd Molar (9-11 years)

1st Molar (9-11 years)

Cuspid (10-12 years)

Lateral Incisor (7-8 years)

Central
Incisors
(6-7 years)

ADULT TEETH
(Ages Usually Emerging)

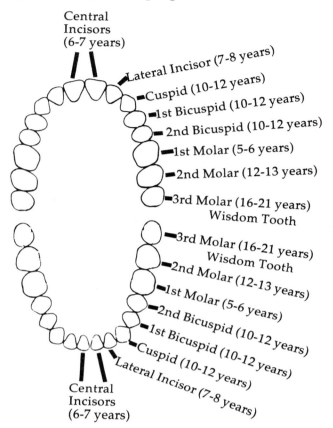

Central
Incisors
(6-7 years)

Lateral Incisor (7-8 years)

Cuspid (10-12 years)

1st Bicuspid (10-12 years)

2nd Bicuspid (10-12 years)

1st Molar (5-6 years)

2nd Molar (12-13 years)

3rd Molar (16-21 years)
Wisdom Tooth

3rd Molar (16-21 years)
Wisdom Tooth

2nd Molar (12-13 years)

1st Molar (5-6 years)

2nd Bicuspid (10-12 years)

1st Bicuspid (10-12 years)

Cuspid (10-12 years)

Lateral Incisor (7-8 years)

Central
Incisors
(6-7 years)

DENTAL RECORD

Date	Age	Treatment

Date	Age	Treatment

CHILD 4

Name _____

Date of Birth _____ Weight at Birth _____ Length at Birth _____ Blood Type _____ Rh Factor _____

Mother's health during pregnancy _____

Delivery complications _____

Place of Birth: Hospital _____ City _____ State _____ Birth Record Filed: _____

Condition of child at birth _____

Type of feeding _____ Age on solid foods _____ Age walking _____ Age talking _____

Immunizations	Date	Immunizations	Date	Immunizations	Date
Two months		12-15 months		10 years	
Polio, Type _____		Measles or M/M/R _____		Rubella _____	
DPT #1 _____		18 Months		Tetanus booster _____	
Four months		Polio booster _____		15 years	
Polio, Type _____		DPT booster _____		DT booster _____	
DPT #2 _____		Five years		20 years	
Six months		Polio booster _____		Tetanus booster _____	
Polio, Type _____		DT booster _____			
DPT #3 _____					

116

IMMUNIZATION – DEFINITIONS

Polio - Sabin oral type (OPV)
      - Salk injected type (IPV)
DPT - Diptheria/Pertussis/Tetanus
      Pertussis - Whooping Cough
      Tetanus - Lockjaw

DT - Diptheria/Tetanus
M/M/R - Measles/Mumps/Rubella
Rubella - German (3-day) Measles

Physical Condition (birth defects, limitations from injury or disease)

_____

_____

_____

ALLERGIES:

To medicines (list): _____

To foods (list): _____

To chemicals or cleansers (list): _____

To substances (Hay Fever): _____

Other (list): _____

VISION:

	At Age 3 Years	At Age 6 Years
Left Eye (OS)		
Near Sighted (myopia)	☐	☐
Far Sighted (hyperopia)	☐	☐
Right Eye (OD)		
Near Sighted (myopia)	☐	☐
Far Sighted (hyperopia)	☐	☐

LEFT EYE

Check

- [ ] Astigmatism
- [ ] Crossed eyes (strabismus)
- [ ] Prism
- [ ] Other (list): _____

RIGHT EYE

Check

- [ ] Astigmatism
- [ ] Crossed eyes (strabismus)
- [ ] Prism
- [ ] Other (list): _____

REFRACTION (Transfer from Eye Doctor's Prescription)

Date	Eye	Sphere	Cylinder	Axis	Prism
	OS				
	OD				
Add for near:			Add for intermediate:		
Date	Eye	Sphere	Cylinder	Axis	Prism
	OS				
	OD				
Add for near:			Add for intermediate:		
Date	Eye	Sphere	Cylinder	Axis	Prism
	OS				
	OD				
Add for near:			Add for intermediate:		
Date	Eye	Sphere	Cylinder	Axis	Prism
	OS				
	OD				
Add for near:			Add for intermediate:		
Date	Eye	Sphere	Cylinder	Axis	Prism
	OS				
	OD				
Add for near:			Add for intermediate:		

LABORATORY TESTS

Have any of these procedures produced a *not* normal result? If so, please note below:

Test	Date	Doctor	Result	Treatment
Blood				
Complete Blood Count (CBC)				
Hemoglobin				
Hematocrit				
White Blood Count (WBC)				
Differential				
Red Blood Count				
Sedimentation Rate				
Blood Chemistry				
Glucose				
Triglicerides				
Cholesterol				
Uric Acid				
Other (list)				
Urinalysis				
Albumin				
Glucose				
White Blood Corpuscles				
Red Blood Corpuscles				
Specific Gravity				
Other (list)				

HEARING

Left Ear	Condition	Right Ear	Condition
At age 18 months	_____	At age 18 months	_____
At age 5 years	_____	At age 5 years	_____
Date: _____	_____	Date: _____	_____
Date: _____	_____	Date: _____	_____
Date: _____	_____	Date: _____	_____
Date: _____	_____	Date: _____	_____

CHILDHOOD DISEASES

Condition	Date	Complications
Chickenpox	_____	_____
German Measles (Rubella)	_____	_____
Infectious Mononucleosis	_____	_____
Measles (Rubeola)	_____	_____
Meningitis	_____	_____
Rheumatic Fever	_____	_____
Roseola	_____	_____
Scarlet Fever	_____	_____
Strep Throat	_____	_____
Other (list) _____	_____	_____
_____	_____	_____
_____	_____	_____
_____	_____	_____
_____	_____	_____
_____	_____	_____
_____	_____	_____
_____	_____	_____

EKG				
X-Rays (list)				
Tuberculin Test				
Other (list)				

MEDICAL RECORD

Date	Doctor	Diagnosis	Treatment	Residual Complications

PRESCRIPTION DRUG RECORD

Date	Drug	Doctor	Result	Adverse Reaction or Allergy

PRESCRIPTION DRUG RECORD

Date	Drug	Doctor	Result	Adverse Reaction or Allergy

BABY TEETH
(Ages Usually Lost)

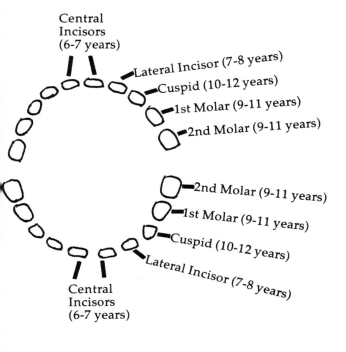

Central
Incisors
(6-7 years)

Lateral Incisor (7-8 years)

Cuspid (10-12 years)

1st Molar (9-11 years)

2nd Molar (9-11 years)

2nd Molar (9-11 years)

1st Molar (9-11 years)

Cuspid (10-12 years)

Lateral Incisor (7-8 years)

Central
Incisors
(6-7 years)

ADULT TEETH
(Ages Usually Emerging)

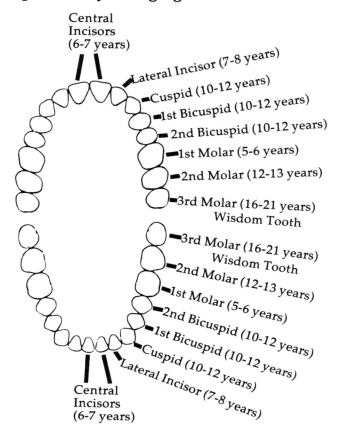

Central
Incisors
(6-7 years)

Lateral Incisor (7-8 years)

Cuspid (10-12 years)

1st Bicuspid (10-12 years)

2nd Bicuspid (10-12 years)

1st Molar (5-6 years)

2nd Molar (12-13 years)

3rd Molar (16-21 years)
Wisdom Tooth

3rd Molar (16-21 years)
Wisdom Tooth

2nd Molar (12-13 years)

1st Molar (5-6 years)

2nd Bicuspid (10-12 years)

1st Bicuspid (10-12 years)

Cuspid (10-12 years)

Lateral Incisor (7-8 years)

Central
Incisors
(6-7 years)

DENTAL RECORD

Date	Age	Treatment

Date	Age	Treatment

CHILD 5

Name _____

Date of Birth _____ Weight at Birth _____ Length at Birth _____ Blood Type _____ Rh Factor _____

Mother's health during pregnancy _____

Delivery complications _____

Place of Birth: Hospital _____ City _____ State _____ Birth Record Filed: _____

Condition of child at birth _____

Type of feeding _____ Age on solid foods _____ Age walking _____ Age talking _____

Immunizations	Date	Immunizations	Date	Immunizations	Date
Two months		12-15 months		10 years	
Polio, Type _____		Measles or M/M/R _____		Rubella _____	
DPT #1 _____		18 Months		Tetanus booster _____	
Four months		Polio booster _____		15 years	
Polio, Type _____		DPT booster _____		DT booster _____	
DPT #2 _____		Five years		20 years	
Six months		Polio booster _____		Tetanus booster _____	
Polio, Type _____		DT booster _____			
DPT #3 _____					

IMMUNIZATION – DEFINITIONS

Polio - Sabin oral type (OPV)   DT - Diptheria/Tetanus

     - Salk injected type (IPV)   M/M/R - Measles/Mumps/Rubella

DPT - Diptheria/Pertussis/Tetanus   Rubella - German (3-day) Measles

     Pertussis - Whooping Cough

     Tetanus - Lockjaw

Physical Condition (birth defects, limitations from injury or disease)

_____

_____

_____

ALLERGIES:

To medicines (list): _____

To foods (list): _____

To chemicals or cleansers (list): _____

To substances (Hay Fever): _____

Other (list): _____

VISION:

	At Age 3 Years	At Age 6 Years		At Age 3 Years	At Age 6 Years
Left Eye (OS)			Right Eye (OD)		
Near Sighted (myopia)	☐	☐	Near Sighted (myopia)	☐	☐
Far Sighted (hyperopia)	☐	☐	Far Sighted (hyperopia)	☐	☐

LEFT EYE

Check

☐ Astigmatism
☐ Crossed eyes (strabismus)
☐ Prism
☐ Other (list): _____

_____

_____

RIGHT EYE

Check

☐ Astigmatism
☐ Crossed eyes (strabismus)
☐ Prism
☐ Other (list): _____

_____

_____

REFRACTION (Transfer from Eye Doctor's Prescription)

Date	Eye	Sphere	Cylinder	Axis	Prism
	OS				
	OD				
Add for near:			Add for intermediate:		
Date	Eye	Sphere	Cylinder	Axis	Prism
	OS				
	OD				
Add for near:			Add for intermediate:		
Date	Eye	Sphere	Cylinder	Axis	Prism
	OS				
	OD				
Add for near:			Add for intermediate:		
Date	Eye	Sphere	Cylinder	Axis	Prism
	OS				
	OD				
Add for near:			Add for intermediate:		
Date	Eye	Sphere	Cylinder	Axis	Prism
	OS				
	OD				
Add for near:			Add for intermediate:		

Date	Eye	Sphere	Cylinder	Axis	Prism
	OS				
	OD				
Add for near:			Add for intermediate:		
Date	Eye	Sphere	Cylinder	Axis	Prism
	OS				
	OD				
Add for near:			Add for intermediate:		
Date	Eye	Sphere	Cylinder	Axis	Prism
	OS				
	OD				
Add for near:			Add for intermediate:		
Date	Eye	Sphere	Cylinder	Axis	Prism
	OS				
	OD				
Add for near:			Add for intermediate:		
Date	Eye	Sphere	Cylinder	Axis	Prism
	OS				
	OD				
Add for near:			Add for intermediate:		

LABORATORY TESTS

Have any of these procedures produced a *not* normal result? If so, please note below:

Test	Date	Doctor	Result	Treatment
Blood				
Complete Blood Count (CBC)				
Hemoglobin				
Hematocrit				
White Blood Count (WBC)				
Differential				
Red Blood Count				
Sedimentation Rate				
Blood Chemistry				
Glucose				
Triglicerides				
Cholesterol				
Uric Acid				
Other (list)				
Urinalysis				
Albumin				
Glucose				
White Blood Corpuscles				
Red Blood Corpuscles				
Specific Gravity				
Other (list)				

HEARING

Left Ear	Condition	Right Ear	Condition
At age 18 months	_____	At age 18 months	_____
At age 5 years	_____	At age 5 years	_____
Date: _____	_____	Date: _____	_____
Date: _____	_____	Date: _____	_____
Date: _____	_____	Date: _____	_____
Date: _____	_____	Date: _____	_____

CHILDHOOD DISEASES

Condition	Date	Complications
Chickenpox	_____	_____
German Measles (Rubella)	_____	_____
Infectious Mononucleosis	_____	_____
Measles (Rubeola)	_____	_____
Meningitis	_____	_____
Rheumatic Fever	_____	_____
Roseola	_____	_____
Scarlet Fever	_____	_____
Strep Throat	_____	_____
Other (list) _____	_____	_____
_____	_____	_____
_____	_____	_____
_____	_____	_____
_____	_____	_____
_____	_____	_____
_____	_____	_____
_____	_____	_____

EKG				
X-Rays (list)				
Tuberculin Test				
Other (list)				

MEDICAL RECORD

Date	Doctor	Diagnosis	Treatment	Residual Complications

PRESCRIPTION DRUG RECORD

Date	Drug	Doctor	Result	Adverse Reaction or Allergy

PRESCRIPTION DRUG RECORD

Date	Drug	Doctor	Result	Adverse Reaction or Allergy

BABY TEETH
(Ages Usually Lost)

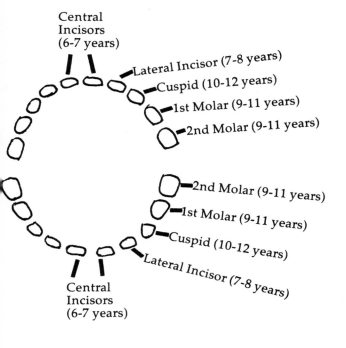

Central
Incisors
(6-7 years)

Lateral Incisor (7-8 years)
Cuspid (10-12 years)
1st Molar (9-11 years)
2nd Molar (9-11 years)

2nd Molar (9-11 years)
1st Molar (9-11 years)
Cuspid (10-12 years)
Lateral Incisor (7-8 years)

Central
Incisors
(6-7 years)

ADULT TEETH
(Ages Usually Emerging)

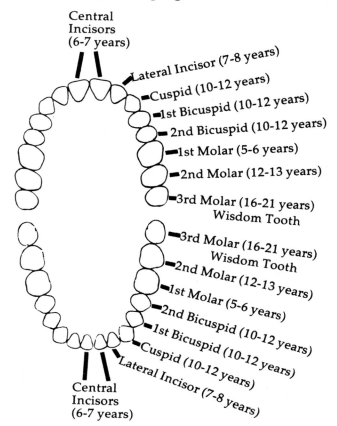

Central
Incisors
(6-7 years)

Lateral Incisor (7-8 years)
Cuspid (10-12 years)
1st Bicuspid (10-12 years)
2nd Bicuspid (10-12 years)
1st Molar (5-6 years)
2nd Molar (12-13 years)
3rd Molar (16-21 years)
Wisdom Tooth

3rd Molar (16-21 years)
Wisdom Tooth
2nd Molar (12-13 years)
1st Molar (5-6 years)
2nd Bicuspid (10-12 years)
1st Bicuspid (10-12 years)
Cuspid (10-12 years)
Lateral Incisor (7-8 years)

Central
Incisors
(6-7 years)

DENTAL RECORD

Date	Age	Treatment

Date	Age	Treatment

CHILD 6

Name ————————————————————

Date of Birth ———————— Weight at Birth ———————— Length at Birth ———————— Blood Type ———————— Rh Factor ————————

Mother's health during pregnancy ————————————————————

Delivery complications ————————————————————

Place of Birth: Hospital ———————— City ———————— State ———————— Birth Record Filed: ————————

Condition of child at birth ————————————————————

Type of feeding ———————— Age on solid foods ———————— Age walking ———————— Age talking ————————

Immunizations	Date	Immunizations	Date	Immunizations	Date
Two months		12-15 months		10 years	
Polio, Type ————		Measles or M/M/R ————		Rubella ————	
DPT #1 ————		18 Months		Tetanus booster ————	
Four months		Polio booster ————		15 years	
Polio, Type ————		DPT booster ————		DT booster ————	
DPT #2 ————		Five years		20 years	
Six months		Polio booster ————		Tetanus booster ————	
Polio, Type ————		DT booster ————			
DPT #3 ————					

IMMUNIZATION – DEFINITIONS

Polio - Sabin oral type (OPV)

 - Salk injected type (IPV)

DPT - Diptheria/Pertussis/Tetanus

  Pertussis - Whooping Cough

  Tetanus - Lockjaw

DT - Diptheria/Tetanus

M/M/R - Measles/Mumps/Rubella

Rubella - German (3-day) Measles

Physical Condition (birth defects, limitations from injury or disease)

_____

_____

_____

ALLERGIES:

To medicines (list): _____

To foods (list): _____

To chemicals or cleansers (list): _____

To substances (Hay Fever): _____

Other (list): _____

VISION:

	At Age 3 Years	At Age 6 Years
Left Eye (OS)		
Near Sighted (myopia)	☐	☐
Far Sighted (hyperopia)	☐	☐

	At Age 3 Years	At Age 6 Years
Right Eye (OD)		
Near Sighted (myopia)	☐	☐
Far Sighted (hyperopia)	☐	☐

LEFT EYE

Check

☐ Astigmatism

☐ Crossed eyes (strabismus)

☐ Prism

☐ Other (list): _____

_____

_____

_____

RIGHT EYE

Check

☐ Astigmatism

☐ Crossed eyes (strabismus)

☐ Prism

☐ Other (list): _____

_____

_____

_____

REFRACTION (Transfer from Eye Doctor's Prescription)

Date	Eye	Sphere	Cylinder	Axis	Prism
	OS				
	OD				
Add for near:			Add for intermediate:		

Date	Eye	Sphere	Cylinder	Axis	Prism
	OS				
	OD				
Add for near:			Add for intermediate:		

Date	Eye	Sphere	Cylinder	Axis	Prism
	OS				
	OD				
Add for near:			Add for intermediate:		

Date	Eye	Sphere	Cylinder	Axis	Prism
	OS				
	OD				
Add for near:			Add for intermediate:		

Date	Eye	Sphere	Cylinder	Axis	Prism
	OS				
	OD				
Add for near:			Add for intermediate:		

138

LABORATORY TESTS

Have any of these procedures produced a *not* normal result? If so, please note below:

Test	Date	Doctor	Result	Treatment
Blood				
Complete Blood Count (CBC)				
Hemoglobin				
Hematocrit				
White Blood Count (WBC)				
Differential				
Red Blood Count				
Sedimentation Rate				
Blood Chemistry				
Glucose				
Triglicerides				
Cholesterol				
Uric Acid				
Other (list)				
Urinalysis				
Albumin				
Glucose				
White Blood Corpuscles				
Red Blood Corpuscles				
Specific Gravity				
Other (list)				

HEARING

Left Ear	Condition	Right Ear	Condition
At age 18 months	_____	At age 18 months	_____
At age 5 years	_____	At age 5 years	_____
Date: _____	_____	Date: _____	_____
Date: _____	_____	Date: _____	_____
Date: _____	_____	Date: _____	_____
Date: _____	_____	Date: _____	_____

CHILDHOOD DISEASES

Condition	Date	Complications
Chickenpox	_____	_____
German Measles (Rubella)	_____	_____
Infectious Mononucleosis	_____	_____
Measles (Rubeola)	_____	_____
Meningitis	_____	_____
Rheumatic Fever	_____	_____
Roseola	_____	_____
Scarlet Fever	_____	_____
Strep Throat	_____	_____
Other (list) _____	_____	_____
_____	_____	_____
_____	_____	_____
_____	_____	_____
_____	_____	_____
_____	_____	_____
_____	_____	_____

EKG				
X-Rays (list)				
Tuberculin Test				
Other (list)				

MEDICAL RECORD

Date	Doctor	Diagnosis	Treatment	Residual Complications

PRESCRIPTION DRUG RECORD

Date	Drug	Doctor	Result	Adverse Reaction or Allergy

PRESCRIPTION DRUG RECORD

Date	Drug	Doctor	Result	Adverse Reaction or Allergy

BABY TEETH
(Ages Usually Lost)

Central Incisors (6-7 years)

Lateral Incisor (7-8 years)

Cuspid (10-12 years)

1st Molar (9-11 years)

2nd Molar (9-11 years)

2nd Molar (9-11 years)

1st Molar (9-11 years)

Cuspid (10-12 years)

Lateral Incisor (7-8 years)

Central Incisors (6-7 years)

ADULT TEETH
(Ages Usually Emerging)

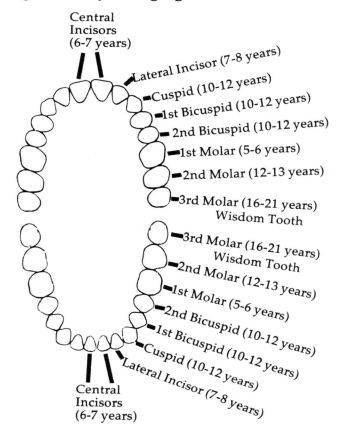

Central Incisors (6-7 years)

Lateral Incisor (7-8 years)

Cuspid (10-12 years)

1st Bicuspid (10-12 years)

2nd Bicuspid (10-12 years)

1st Molar (5-6 years)

2nd Molar (12-13 years)

3rd Molar (16-21 years) Wisdom Tooth

3rd Molar (16-21 years) Wisdom Tooth

2nd Molar (12-13 years)

1st Molar (5-6 years)

2nd Bicuspid (10-12 years)

1st Bicuspid (10-12 years)

Cuspid (10-12 years)

Lateral Incisor (7-8 years)

Central Incisors (6-7 years)

DENTAL RECORD

Date	Age	Treatment

Date	Age	Treatment

CHILD 7

Name _____

Date of Birth _____ Weight at Birth _____ Length at Birth _____ Blood Type _____ Rh Factor _____

Mother's health during pregnancy _____

Delivery complications _____

Place of Birth: Hospital _____ City _____ State _____ Birth Record Filed: _____

Condition of child at birth _____

Type of feeding _____ Age on solid foods _____ Age walking _____ Age talking _____

Immunizations	Date	Immunizations	Date	Immunizations	Date
Two months		12-15 months		10 years	
Polio, Type ___		Measles or M/M/R		Rubella	
DPT #1		18 Months		Tetanus booster	
Four months		Polio booster		15 years	
Polio, Type ___		DPT booster		DT booster	
DPT #2		Five years		20 years	
Six months		Polio booster		Tetanus booster	
Polio, Type ___		DT booster			
DPT #3					

IMMUNIZATION – DEFINITIONS

Polio - Sabin oral type (OPV)　　　　　DT - Diptheria/Tetanus
　　　 - Salk injected type (IPV)　　　　M/M/R - Measles/Mumps/Rubella
DPT - Diptheria/Pertussis/Tetanus　　Rubella - German (3-day) Measles
　　　　Pertussis - Whooping Cough
　　　　Tetanus - Lockjaw

Physical Condition (birth defects, limitations from injury or disease)

_____

_____

_____

ALLERGIES:

To medicines (list): _____

To foods (list): _____

To chemicals or cleansers (list): _____

To substances (Hay Fever): _____

Other (list): _____

VISION:

Left Eye (OS)	At Age 3 Years	At Age 6 Years
Near Sighted (myopia)	[ ]	[ ]
Far Sighted (hyperopia)	[ ]	[ ]

Right Eye (OD)	At Age 3 Years	At Age 6 Years
Near Sighted (myopia)	[ ]	[ ]
Far Sighted (hyperopia)	[ ]	[ ]

LEFT EYE

Check

- [ ] Astigmatism
- [ ] Crossed eyes (strabismus)
- [ ] Prism
- [ ] Other (list): _____

_____

_____

_____

RIGHT EYE

Check

- [ ] Astigmatism
- [ ] Crossed eyes (strabismus)
- [ ] Prism
- [ ] Other (list): _____

_____

_____

_____

REFRACTION (Transfer from Eye Doctor's Prescription)

Date	Eye	Sphere	Cylinder	Axis	Prism
	OS				
	OD				
Add for near:			Add for intermediate:		

Date	Eye	Sphere	Cylinder	Axis	Prism
	OS				
	OD				
Add for near:			Add for intermediate:		

Date	Eye	Sphere	Cylinder	Axis	Prism
	OS				
	OD				
Add for near:			Add for intermediate:		

Date	Eye	Sphere	Cylinder	Axis	Prism
	OS				
	OD				
Add for near:			Add for intermediate:		

Date	Eye	Sphere	Cylinder	Axis	Prism
	OS				
	OD				
Add for near:			Add for intermediate:		

148

LABORATORY TESTS

Have any of these procedures produced a *not* normal result? If so, please note below:

Test	Date	Doctor	Result	Treatment
Blood				
Complete Blood Count (CBC)				
Hemoglobin				
Hematocrit				
White Blood Count (WBC)				
Differential				
Red Blood Count				
Sedimentation Rate				
Blood Chemistry				
Glucose				
Triglicerides				
Cholesterol				
Uric Acid				
Other (list)				
Urinalysis				
Albumin				
Glucose				
White Blood Corpuscles				
Red Blood Corpuscles				
Specific Gravity				
Other (list)				

HEARING

Left Ear	Condition	Right Ear	Condition
At age 18 months	_____	At age 18 months	_____
At age 5 years	_____	At age 5 years	_____
Date: _____	_____	Date: _____	_____
Date: _____	_____	Date: _____	_____
Date: _____	_____	Date: _____	_____
Date: _____	_____	Date: _____	_____

CHILDHOOD DISEASES

Condition	Date	Complications
Chickenpox	_____	_____
German Measles (Rubella)	_____	_____
Infectious Mononucleosis	_____	_____
Measles (Rubeola)	_____	_____
Meningitis	_____	_____
Rheumatic Fever	_____	_____
Roseola	_____	_____
Scarlet Fever	_____	_____
Strep Throat	_____	_____
Other (list) _____	_____	_____
_____	_____	_____
_____	_____	_____
_____	_____	_____
_____	_____	_____
_____	_____	_____
_____	_____	_____
_____	_____	_____

EKG				
X-Rays (list)				
Tuberculin Test				
Other (list)				

MEDICAL RECORD

Date	Doctor	Diagnosis	Treatment	Residual Complications

PRESCRIPTION DRUG RECORD

Date	Drug	Doctor	Result	Adverse Reaction or Allergy

PRESCRIPTION DRUG RECORD

Date	Drug	Doctor	Result	Adverse Reaction or Allergy

BABY TEETH
(Ages Usually Lost)

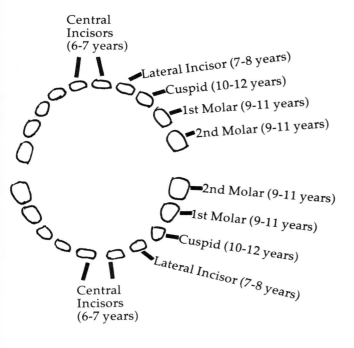

Central Incisors (6-7 years)

Lateral Incisor (7-8 years)
Cuspid (10-12 years)
1st Molar (9-11 years)
2nd Molar (9-11 years)

2nd Molar (9-11 years)
1st Molar (9-11 years)
Cuspid (10-12 years)
Lateral Incisor (7-8 years)

Central Incisors (6-7 years)

ADULT TEETH
(Ages Usually Emerging)

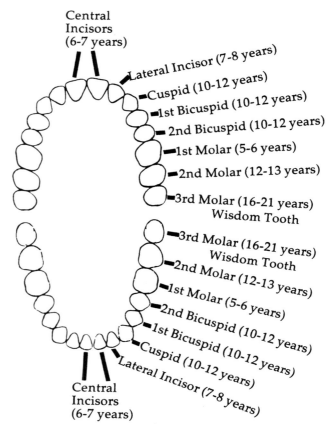

Central Incisors (6-7 years)

Lateral Incisor (7-8 years)
Cuspid (10-12 years)
1st Bicuspid (10-12 years)
2nd Bicuspid (10-12 years)
1st Molar (5-6 years)
2nd Molar (12-13 years)
3rd Molar (16-21 years) Wisdom Tooth

3rd Molar (16-21 years) Wisdom Tooth
2nd Molar (12-13 years)
1st Molar (5-6 years)
2nd Bicuspid (10-12 years)
1st Bicuspid (10-12 years)
Cuspid (10-12 years)
Lateral Incisor (7-8 years)

Central Incisors (6-7 years)

DENTAL RECORD

Date	Age	Treatment

Date	Age	Treatment

MATERNAL GRANDMOTHER (Mother's Mother)

Name _____

Street Address _____ Apt. No. _____ City _____ State _____ ZIP _____

Date of Birth ___/___/___ Place of Birth: City _____ State _____ Country _____

If deceased, Date of Death _____ Cause of Death: _____

MEDICAL HISTORY

	Check	Age	Result
Alcohol or Drug Problem	☐	_____	_____
Allergies (list)			
_____	☐	_____	_____
_____	☐	_____	_____
_____	☐	_____	_____
Asthma	☐	_____	_____
Cancer	☐	_____	_____
Color Blindness	☐	_____	_____
Diabetes	☐	_____	_____
Gout	☐	_____	_____
Heart Problems	☐	_____	_____
Hemophilia	☐	_____	_____
Hypertension (High Blood Pressure)	☐	_____	_____
Hysterectomy	☐	_____	_____
Leukemia	☐	_____	_____
Mastectomy	☐	_____	_____
Mental or Emotional Problem	☐	_____	_____
Sickle Cell Anemia	☐	_____	_____
Stroke	☐	_____	_____
Tay-Sachs Gene	☐	_____	_____
Ulcers	☐	_____	_____

	Check	Age	Result
Varicose Veins	☐	_____	_____
Other (list)			
_____	☐	_____	_____
_____	☐	_____	_____
_____	☐	_____	_____

VISION

	Check	Age
Myopia (nearsighted)	☐	_____
Hyperopia (farsighted)	☐	_____
Astigmatism	☐	_____
Presbyopia (inability to focus near)	☐	_____

PHYSICAL DISABILITIES (list)

_____
_____

MAJOR ILLNESSES (list)

_____
_____

Age at Puberty _____
Age at Menopause _____

156

MATERNAL GRANDFATHER (Mother's Father)

Name _____

Street Address _____ Apt. No. _____ City _____ State _____ ZIP _____

Phone _____ Business Phone _____

Date of Birth ___/___/___ Place of Birth: City _____ State _____ Country _____

If deceased, Date of Death ___/___/___ Cause of Death: _____

MEDICAL HISTORY

	Check	Age	Result
Alcohol or Drug Problem	☐	_____	_____
Allergies (list)		_____	_____
		_____	_____
		_____	_____
Asthma	☐	_____	_____
Cancer	☐	_____	_____
Color Blindness	☐	_____	_____
Diabetes	☐	_____	_____
Gout	☐	_____	_____
Heart Problems	☐	_____	_____
Hemophilia	☐	_____	_____
Hypertension (High Blood Pressure)	☐	_____	_____
Leukemia	☐	_____	_____
Mental or Emotional Problem	☐	_____	_____
Prostate Trouble	☐	_____	_____
Sickle Cell Anemia	☐	_____	_____
Stroke	☐	_____	_____
Tay-Sachs Gene	☐	_____	_____
Ulcers	☐	_____	_____
Varicose Veins	☐	_____	_____

VISION

	Check	Age	Result
Myopia (nearsighted)	☐	_____	_____
Hyperopia (farsighted)	☐	_____	_____
Astigmatism	☐	_____	_____
Presbyopia (inability to focus near)	☐	_____	_____
Other (list)		_____	_____
		_____	_____

PHYSICAL DISABILITIES (list)

	Age
_____	_____
_____	_____
_____	_____
_____	_____

MAJOR ILLNESSES (list)

	Age
_____	_____
_____	_____
_____	_____
_____	_____

157

PATERNAL GRANDMOTHER (Father's Mother)

Name _____

Street Address _____ Apt. No. _____ City _____ State _____ ZIP _____

Phone _____

Date of Birth _____ Place of Birth: City _____ State _____ Country _____

If deceased, Date of Death ___/___/___ Cause of Death: _____

MEDICAL HISTORY

	Check	Age	Result
Alcohol or Drug Problem	☐	_____	_____
Allergies (list)			
_____			
_____			
Asthma	☐	_____	_____
Cancer	☐	_____	_____
Color Blindness	☐	_____	_____
Diabetes	☐	_____	_____
Gout	☐	_____	_____
Heart Problems	☐	_____	_____
Hemophilia	☐	_____	_____
Hypertension (High Blood Pressure)	☐	_____	_____
Hysterectomy	☐	_____	_____
Leukemia	☐	_____	_____
Mastectomy	☐	_____	_____
Mental or Emotional Problem	☐	_____	_____
Sickle Cell Anemia	☐	_____	_____
Stroke	☐	_____	_____
Tay-Sachs Gene	☐	_____	_____
Ulcers	☐	_____	_____

	Check	Age	Result
Varicose Veins	☐	_____	_____
Other (list)			
_____	☐	_____	_____
_____	☐	_____	_____
_____	☐	_____	_____

VISION

	Check
Myopia (nearsighted)	☐
Hyperopia (farsighted)	☐
Astigmatism	☐
Presbyopia (inability to focus near)	☐

PHYSICAL DISABILITIES (list)

	Age
_____	_____
_____	_____
_____	_____

MAJOR ILLNESSES (list)

	Age
_____	_____
_____	_____
_____	_____

Age at Puberty _____
Age at Menopause _____

PATERNAL GRANDFATHER (Father's Father)

Name _____ Phone _____ Business Phone _____

Street Address _____ Apt. No. _____ City _____ State _____ ZIP _____

Date of Birth ___/___/___ Place of Birth: City _____ State _____ Country _____

If deceased, Date of Death ___/___/___ Cause of Death: _____

MEDICAL HISTORY

	Check	Age	Result
Alcohol or Drug Problem	☐	___	_____
Allergies (list)			
_____		___	_____
_____		___	_____
Asthma	☐	___	_____
Cancer	☐	___	_____
Color Blindness	☐	___	_____
Diabetes	☐	___	_____
Gout	☐	___	_____
Heart Problems	☐	___	_____
Hemophilia	☐	___	_____
Hypertension (High Blood Pressure)	☐	___	_____
Leukemia	☐	___	_____
Mental or Emotional Problem	☐	___	_____
Prostate Trouble	☐	___	_____
Sickle Cell Anemia	☐	___	_____
Stroke	☐	___	_____
Tay-Sachs Gene	☐	___	_____
Ulcers	☐	___	_____
Varicose Veins	☐	___	_____

VISION

	Check	Result
Myopia (nearsighted)	☐	_____
Hyperopia (farsighted)	☐	_____
Astigmatism	☐	_____
Presbyopia (inability to focus near)	☐	_____
Other (list)		

PHYSICAL DISABILITIES (list)

	Age
_____	___
_____	___
_____	___
_____	___

MAJOR ILLNESSES (list)

	Age
_____	___
_____	___
_____	___
_____	___

MATERNAL AUNT or UNCLE (Mother's Aunt or Uncle)

Name _____

Street Address _____ Phone _____ Business Phone _____

Date of Birth _____ Apt. No. ____ City _____ State _____ ZIP _____

Place of Birth: City _____ State _____ Country _____

If deceased, Date of Death _____/_____ Cause of Death: _____

MEDICAL HISTORY

	Check	Age	Result
Alcohol or Drug Problem	☐	_____	_____
Allergies (list)		_____	_____
		_____	_____
		_____	_____
Asthma	☐	_____	_____
Cancer	☐	_____	_____
Color Blindness	☐	_____	_____
Diabetes	☐	_____	_____
Gout	☐	_____	_____
Heart Problems	☐	_____	_____
Hemophilia	☐	_____	_____
Hypertension (High Blood Pressure)	☐	_____	_____
Hysterectomy	☐	_____	_____
Leukemia	☐	_____	_____
Mastectomy	☐	_____	_____
Mental or Emotional Problem	☐	_____	_____
Prostate Trouble	☐	_____	_____
Sickle Cell Anemia	☐	_____	_____
Stroke	☐	_____	_____
Tay-Sachs Gene	☐	_____	_____

	Check	Age	Result
Ulcers	☐	_____	_____
Varicose Veins	☐	_____	_____
Other (list)		_____	_____
	☐	_____	_____
	☐	_____	_____

VISION

	Check	Age
Myopia (nearsighted)		
Hyperopia (farsighted)	☐	_____
Astigmatism	☐	_____
Presbyopia (inability to focus near)	☐	_____

PHYSICAL DISABILITIES (list)

_____
_____
_____

MAJOR ILLNESSES (list)

_____
_____
_____

Aunts only:
Age at Puberty _____
Age at Menopause _____

160

MATERNAL AUNT or UNCLE (Mother's Aunt or Uncle)

Name _____ Phone _____ Business Phone _____

Street Address _____ Apt. No. _____ City _____ State _____ ZIP _____

Date of Birth ___/___/___ Place of Birth: City _____ State _____ Country _____

If deceased, Date of Death ___/___/___ Cause of Death: _____

MEDICAL HISTORY

	Check	Age	Result
Alcohol or Drug Problem	☐		
Allergies (list)	☐	_____	_____
	☐	_____	_____
	☐	_____	_____
	☐	_____	_____
Asthma	☐	_____	_____
Cancer	☐	_____	_____
Color Blindness	☐	_____	_____
Diabetes	☐	_____	_____
Gout	☐	_____	_____
Heart Problems	☐	_____	_____
Hemophilia	☐	_____	_____
Hypertension (High Blood Pressure)	☐	_____	_____
Hysterectomy	☐	_____	_____
Leukemia	☐	_____	_____
Mastectomy	☐	_____	_____
Mental or Emotional Problem	☐	_____	_____
Prostate Trouble	☐	_____	_____
Sickle Cell Anemia	☐	_____	_____
Stroke	☐	_____	_____
Tay-Sachs Gene	☐	_____	_____

	Check	Age	Result
Ulcers	☐	_____	_____
Varicose Veins	☐	_____	_____
Other (list)	☐	_____	_____
	☐	_____	_____

VISION

	Check	Age
Myopia (nearsighted)	☐	
Hyperopia (farsighted)	☐	
Astigmatism	☐	
Presbyopia (inability to focus near)	☐	

PHYSICAL DISABILITIES (list)

_____

_____

MAJOR ILLNESSES (list)

_____

_____

Aunts only:

Age at Puberty _____

Age at Menopause _____

161

MATERNAL AUNT or UNCLE (Mother's Aunt or Uncle)

Name _____

Street Address _____ Apt. No. _____ Phone _____ Business Phone _____

Date of Birth __/__/__ Place of Birth: City _____ City _____ State _____ State _____ ZIP _____ Country _____

If deceased, Date of Death __/__/__ Cause of Death: _____

MEDICAL HISTORY

	Check	Age	Result
Alcohol or Drug Problem	☐	____	_____
Allergies (list)	☐	____	_____
	☐	____	_____
	☐	____	_____
Asthma	☐	____	_____
Cancer	☐	____	_____
Color Blindness	☐	____	_____
Diabetes	☐	____	_____
Gout	☐	____	_____
Heart Problems	☐	____	_____
Hemophilia	☐	____	_____
Hypertension (High Blood Pressure)	☐	____	_____
Hysterectomy	☐	____	_____
Leukemia	☐	____	_____
Mastectomy	☐	____	_____
Mental or Emotional Problem	☐	____	_____
Prostate Trouble	☐	____	_____
Sickle Cell Anemia	☐	____	_____
Stroke	☐	____	_____
Tay-Sachs Gene	☐	____	_____

	Check	Age	Result
Ulcers	☐	____	_____
Varicose Veins	☐	____	_____
Other (list)	☐	____	_____
	☐	____	_____

VISION

	Check	Age	Result
Myopia (nearsighted)	☐	____	_____
Hyperopia (farsighted)	☐	____	_____
Astigmatism	☐	____	_____
Presbyopia (inability to focus near)	☐	____	_____

PHYSICAL DISABILITIES (list)

_____

_____

MAJOR ILLNESSES (list)

_____

_____

Aunts only:

Age at Puberty _____

Age at Menopause _____

162

MATERNAL AUNT or UNCLE (Mother's Aunt or Uncle)

Name _____

Street Address _____

Date of Birth ___/___/___   Place of Birth: City _____ State _____ Country _____

    Apt. No. _____   Phone _____   Business Phone _____

    City _____ State _____ ZIP _____

If deceased, Date of Death _____ Cause of Death: _____

MEDICAL HISTORY

	Check	Age	Result
Alcohol or Drug Problem	☐		
Allergies (list)	☐		
	☐		
	☐		
Asthma	☐		
Cancer	☐		
Color Blindness	☐		
Diabetes	☐		
Gout	☐		
Heart Problems	☐		
Hemophilia	☐		
Hypertension (High Blood Pressure)	☐		
Hysterectomy	☐		
Leukemia	☐		
Mastectomy	☐		
Mental or Emotional Problem	☐		
Prostate Trouble	☐		
Sickle Cell Anemia	☐		
Stroke	☐		
Tay-Sachs Gene	☐		

	Check	Age	Result
Ulcers	☐		
Varicose Veins	☐		
Other (list)	☐		
	☐		

VISION

	Check	Age
Myopia (nearsighted)	☐	
Hyperopia (farsighted)	☐	
Astigmatism	☐	
Presbyopia (inability to focus near)	☐	

PHYSICAL DISABILITIES (list)

_____

_____

MAJOR ILLNESSES (list)

_____

_____

Aunts only:

Age at Puberty _____

Age at Menopause _____

163

PATERNAL AUNT or UNCLE (Father's Aunt or Uncle)

Name _____

Street Address _____ Apt. No. _____ City _____ State _____ Business Phone _____

Date of Birth ___/___/___ Place of Birth: City _____ State _____ Country _____ Phone _____ ZIP _____

If deceased, Date of Death ___/___/___ Cause of Death: _____

MEDICAL HISTORY

	Check	Age	Result
Alcohol or Drug Problem	☐	_____	_____
Allergies (list)		_____	_____
		_____	_____
		_____	_____
Asthma	☐	_____	_____
Cancer	☐	_____	_____
Color Blindness	☐	_____	_____
Diabetes	☐	_____	_____
Gout	☐	_____	_____
Heart Problems	☐	_____	_____
Hemophilia	☐	_____	_____
Hypertension (High Blood Pressure)	☐	_____	_____
Hysterectomy	☐	_____	_____
Leukemia	☐	_____	_____
Mastectomy	☐	_____	_____
Mental or Emotional Problem	☐	_____	_____
Prostate Trouble	☐	_____	_____
Sickle Cell Anemia	☐	_____	_____
Stroke	☐	_____	_____
Tay-Sachs Gene	☐	_____	_____

	Check	Age	Result
Ulcers	☐	_____	_____
Varicose Veins	☐	_____	_____
Other (list)	☐	_____	_____
	☐	_____	_____

VISION

	Check
Myopia (nearsighted)	☐
Hyperopia (farsighted)	☐
Astigmatism	☐
Presbyopia (inability to focus near)	☐

PHYSICAL DISABILITIES (list)

Age _____
_____
_____
_____

MAJOR ILLNESSES (list)

Age _____
_____
_____
_____

Aunts only:
Age at Puberty _____
Age at Menopause _____

PATERNAL AUNT or UNCLE (Father's Aunt or Uncle)

Name _____

Street Address _____ Apt. No. _____ City _____ Phone _____ State _____ Business Phone _____ ZIP _____

Date of Birth ___/___/___ Place of Birth: City _____ State _____ Country _____

If deceased, Date of Death _____ Cause of Death: _____

MEDICAL HISTORY

	Check	Age	Result
Alcohol or Drug Problem	☐	_____	_____
Allergies (list)		_____	_____
		_____	_____
		_____	_____
Asthma	☐	_____	_____
Cancer	☐	_____	_____
Color Blindness	☐	_____	_____
Diabetes	☐	_____	_____
Gout	☐	_____	_____
Heart Problems	☐	_____	_____
Hemophilia	☐	_____	_____
Hypertension (High Blood Pressure)	☐	_____	_____
Hysterectomy	☐	_____	_____
Leukemia	☐	_____	_____
Mastectomy	☐	_____	_____
Mental or Emotional Problem	☐	_____	_____
Prostate Trouble	☐	_____	_____
Sickle Cell Anemia	☐	_____	_____
Stroke	☐	_____	_____
Tay-Sachs Gene	☐	_____	_____
Ulcers	☐	_____	_____
Varicose Veins	☐	_____	_____
Other (list)	☐	_____	_____
	☐	_____	_____

VISION

	Check
Myopia (nearsighted)	☐
Hyperopia (farsighted)	☐
Astigmatism	☐
Presbyopia (inability to focus near)	☐

PHYSICAL DISABILITIES (list)

Age
_____ _____
_____ _____

MAJOR ILLNESSES (list)

Age
_____ _____
_____ _____

Aunts only:
Age at Puberty _____
Age at Menopause _____

PATERNAL AUNT or UNCLE (Father's Aunt or Uncle)

Name _____

Street Address _____ Apt. No. ____ City _____ Phone _____ Business Phone _____

Date of Birth ___/___/___ Place of Birth: City _____ State _____ State _____ ZIP _____

If deceased, Date of Death ___/___/___ Cause of Death: _____ Country _____

MEDICAL HISTORY

	Check	Age	Result
Alcohol or Drug Problem	☐	_____	_____
Allergies (list)	☐	_____	_____
_____	☐	_____	_____
_____	☐	_____	_____
Asthma	☐	_____	_____
Cancer	☐	_____	_____
Color Blindness	☐	_____	_____
Diabetes	☐	_____	_____
Gout	☐	_____	_____
Heart Problems	☐	_____	_____
Hemophilia	☐	_____	_____
Hypertension (High Blood Pressure)	☐	_____	_____
Hysterectomy	☐	_____	_____
Leukemia	☐	_____	_____
Mastectomy	☐	_____	_____
Mental or Emotional Problem	☐	_____	_____
Prostate Trouble	☐	_____	_____
Sickle Cell Anemia	☐	_____	_____
Stroke	☐	_____	_____
Tay-Sachs Gene	☐	_____	_____
Ulcers	☐	_____	_____
Varicose Veins	☐	_____	_____
Other (list)	☐	_____	_____
	☐	_____	_____

VISION

	Check	Age
Myopia (nearsighted)	☐	_____
Hyperopia (farsighted)	☐	_____
Astigmatism	☐	_____
Presbyopia (inability to focus near)	☐	_____

PHYSICAL DISABILITIES (list)

_____ Age ____
_____ Age ____

MAJOR ILLNESSES (list)

_____
_____

Aunts only:
Age at Puberty _____
Age at Menopause _____

PATERNAL AUNT or UNCLE (Father's Aunt or Uncle)

Name _____

Street Address _____ Apt. No. _____ City _____ State _____ Business Phone _____

Date of Birth ___/___/___ Place of Birth: City _____ State _____ Country _____ Phone _____ ZIP _____

If deceased, Date of Death ___/___/___ Cause of Death: _____

MEDICAL HISTORY

	Check	Age	Result
Alcohol or Drug Problem	☐	_____	_____
Allergies (list)			
_____	☐	_____	_____
_____	☐	_____	_____
_____	☐	_____	_____
Asthma	☐	_____	_____
Cancer	☐	_____	_____
Color Blindness	☐	_____	_____
Diabetes	☐	_____	_____
Gout	☐	_____	_____
Heart Problems	☐	_____	_____
Hemophilia	☐	_____	_____
Hypertension (High Blood Pressure)	☐	_____	_____
Hysterectomy	☐	_____	_____
Leukemia	☐	_____	_____
Mastectomy	☐	_____	_____
Mental or Emotional Problem	☐	_____	_____
Prostate Trouble	☐	_____	_____
Sickle Cell Anemia	☐	_____	_____
Stroke	☐	_____	_____
Tay-Sachs Gene	☐	_____	_____

	Check	Age	Result
Ulcers	☐	_____	_____
Varicose Veins	☐	_____	_____
Other (list)			
_____	☐	_____	_____
_____	☐	_____	_____

VISION

	Check	Age
Myopia (nearsighted)	☐	_____
Hyperopia (farsighted)	☐	_____
Astigmatism	☐	_____
Presbyopia (inability to focus near)	☐	_____

PHYSICAL DISABILITIES (list)

_____
_____

MAJOR ILLNESSES (list)

_____
_____
_____

Aunts only:
Age at Puberty _____
Age at Menopause _____

167

MATERNAL SIBLING (Mother's Brother or Sister)

Name _____ Phone _____ Business Phone _____

Street Address _____ Apt. No. _____ City _____ State _____ ZIP _____

Date of Birth _____ / _____ / _____ Place of Birth: City _____ State _____ Country _____

If deceased, Date of Death _____ / _____ / _____ Cause of Death: _____

MEDICAL HISTORY

	Check	Age	Result
Alcohol or Drug Problem	☐	_____	_____
Allergies (list) _____	☐	_____	_____
_____	☐	_____	_____
_____	☐	_____	_____
Asthma	☐	_____	_____
Cancer	☐	_____	_____
Color Blindness	☐	_____	_____
Diabetes	☐	_____	_____
Gout	☐	_____	_____
Heart Problems	☐	_____	_____
Hemophilia	☐	_____	_____
Hypertension (High Blood Pressure)	☐	_____	_____
Hysterectomy	☐	_____	_____
Leukemia	☐	_____	_____
Mastectomy	☐	_____	_____
Mental or Emotional Problem	☐	_____	_____
Prostate Trouble	☐	_____	_____
Sickle Cell Anemia	☐	_____	_____
Stroke	☐	_____	_____
Tay-Sachs Gene	☐	_____	_____

	Check	Age	Result
Ulcers	☐	_____	_____
Varicose Veins	☐	_____	_____
Other (list)	☐	_____	_____
_____	☐	_____	_____

VISION

	Check	Age
Myopia (nearsighted)	☐	_____
Hyperopia (farsighted)	☐	_____
Astigmatism	☐	_____
Presbyopia (inability to focus near)	☐	_____

PHYSICAL DISABILITIES (list)

_____

_____

_____

MAJOR ILLNESSES (list)

_____

_____

_____

Aunts only:

Age at Puberty _____

Age at Menopause _____

168

MATERNAL SIBLING (Mother's Brother or Sister)

Name _____

Street Address _____ Apt. No. _____ City _____ State _____ Business Phone _____

Date of Birth _____ / _____ / _____ Place of Birth: City _____ State _____ Phone _____

If deceased, Date of Death _____ Cause of Death: _____ State _____ Country _____ ZIP _____

MEDICAL HISTORY

	Check	Age	Result
Alcohol or Drug Problem	☐		
Allergies (list)			
Asthma	☐		
Cancer	☐		
Color Blindness	☐		
Diabetes	☐		
Gout	☐		
Heart Problems	☐		
Hemophilia	☐		
Hypertension (High Blood Pressure)	☐		
Hysterectomy	☐		
Leukemia	☐		
Mastectomy	☐		
Mental or Emotional Problem	☐		
Prostate Trouble	☐		
Sickle Cell Anemia	☐		
Stroke	☐		
Tay-Sachs Gene	☐		

	Check	Age	Result
Ulcers	☐		
Varicose Veins	☐		
Other (list)	☐		
	☐		

VISION

	Check	Age
Myopia (nearsighted)	☐	
Hyperopia (farsighted)	☐	
Astigmatism	☐	
Presbyopia (inability to focus near)	☐	

PHYSICAL DISABILITIES (list)

_____

_____

_____

MAJOR ILLNESSES (list)

_____

_____

_____

Aunts only:

Age at Puberty _____

Age at Menopause _____

169

MATERNAL SIBLING (Mother's Brother or Sister)

Name _____

Street Address _____ Apt. No. _____ City _____ State _____ Business Phone _____

Date of Birth ___/___/___ Place of Birth: City _____ State _____ Country _____ Phone _____ ZIP _____

If deceased, Date of Death ___/___/___ Cause of Death: _____

MEDICAL HISTORY

	Check	Age	Result
Alcohol or Drug Problem	☐	_____	_____
Allergies (list)			
_____		_____	_____
_____		_____	_____
Asthma	☐	_____	_____
Cancer	☐	_____	_____
Color Blindness	☐	_____	_____
Diabetes	☐	_____	_____
Gout	☐	_____	_____
Heart Problems	☐	_____	_____
Hemophilia	☐	_____	_____
Hypertension (High Blood Pressure)	☐	_____	_____
Hysterectomy	☐	_____	_____
Leukemia	☐	_____	_____
Mastectomy	☐	_____	_____
Mental or Emotional Problem	☐	_____	_____
Prostate Trouble	☐	_____	_____
Sickle Cell Anemia	☐	_____	_____
Stroke	☐	_____	_____
Tay-Sachs Gene	☐	_____	_____

	Check	Age	Result
Ulcers	☐	_____	_____
Varicose Veins	☐	_____	_____
Other (list)			
_____	☐	_____	_____
_____	☐	_____	_____

VISION

	Check
Myopia (nearsighted)	☐
Hyperopia (farsighted)	☐
Astigmatism	☐
Presbyopia (inability to focus near)	☐

PHYSICAL DISABILITIES (list)

_____ Age _____

_____ _____

_____ _____

MAJOR ILLNESSES (list)

_____ Age _____

_____ _____

_____ _____

Aunts only:

Age at Puberty _____

Age at Menopause _____

MATERNAL SIBLING (Mother's Brother or Sister)

Name _____ Phone _____ Business Phone _____

Street Address _____ Apt. No. _____ City _____ State _____ ZIP _____

Date of Birth ___/___/___ Place of Birth: City _____ State _____ Country _____

If deceased, Date of Death ___/___/___ Cause of Death: _____

MEDICAL HISTORY

	Check	Age	Result
Alcohol or Drug Problem	☐	___	___
Allergies (list)	☐	___	___
___	☐	___	___
___	☐	___	___
Asthma	☐	___	___
Cancer	☐	___	___
Color Blindness	☐	___	___
Diabetes	☐	___	___
Gout	☐	___	___
Heart Problems	☐	___	___
Hemophilia	☐	___	___
Hypertension (High Blood Pressure)	☐	___	___
Hysterectomy	☐	___	___
Leukemia	☐	___	___
Mastectomy	☐	___	___
Mental or Emotional Problem	☐	___	___
Prostate Trouble	☐	___	___
Sickle Cell Anemia	☐	___	___
Stroke	☐	___	___
Tay-Sachs Gene	☐	___	___
Ulcers	☐	___	___
Varicose Veins	☐	___	___
Other (list)	☐	___	___
___	☐	___	___

VISION

	Check	Age
Myopia (nearsighted)	☐	___
Hyperopia (farsighted)	☐	___
Astigmatism	☐	___
Presbyopia (inability to focus near)	☐	___

PHYSICAL DISABILITIES (list)

_____
_____
_____

MAJOR ILLNESSES (list)

_____
_____
_____

Aunts only:
Age at Puberty _____
Age at Menopause _____

171

PATERNAL SIBLING (Father's Brother or Sister)

Name _____

Street Address _____ Apt. No. _____ City _____ State _____ ZIP _____

Date of Birth ___/___/___ Place of Birth: City _____ State _____ Country _____

Phone _____ Business Phone _____

If deceased, Date of Death ___/___/___ Cause of Death: _____

MEDICAL HISTORY

	Check	Age	Result
Alcohol or Drug Problem	☐	_____	_____
Allergies (list)			
_____	☐	_____	_____
_____	☐	_____	_____
_____	☐	_____	_____
Asthma	☐	_____	_____
Cancer	☐	_____	_____
Color Blindness	☐	_____	_____
Diabetes	☐	_____	_____
Gout	☐	_____	_____
Heart Problems	☐	_____	_____
Hemophilia	☐	_____	_____
Hypertension (High Blood Pressure)	☐	_____	_____
Hysterectomy	☐	_____	_____
Leukemia	☐	_____	_____
Mastectomy	☐	_____	_____
Mental or Emotional Problem	☐	_____	_____
Prostate Trouble	☐	_____	_____
Sickle Cell Anemia	☐	_____	_____
Stroke	☐	_____	_____
Tay-Sachs Gene	☐	_____	_____
Ulcers	☐	_____	_____
Varicose Veins	☐	_____	_____
Other (list)			
_____	☐	_____	_____
_____	☐	_____	_____

VISION

	Check	Result
Myopia (nearsighted)	☐	_____
Hyperopia (farsighted)	☐	_____
Astigmatism	☐	_____
Presbyopia (inability to focus near)	☐	_____

PHYSICAL DISABILITIES (list)

	Age
_____	_____
_____	_____
_____	_____

MAJOR ILLNESSES (list)

	Age
_____	_____
_____	_____
_____	_____

Aunts only:

Age at Puberty _____

Age at Menopause _____

PATERNAL SIBLING (Father's Brother or Sister)

Name _____ Phone _____ Business Phone _____

Street Address _____ Apt. No. _____ City _____ State _____ ZIP _____

Date of Birth ___/___/___ Place of Birth: City _____ State _____ Country _____

If deceased, Date of Death ___/___/___ Cause of Death: _____

MEDICAL HISTORY

	Check	Age	Result
Alcohol or Drug Problem	☐	___	_____
Allergies (list)			
_____	☐	___	_____
_____	☐	___	_____
_____	☐	___	_____
Asthma	☐	___	_____
Cancer	☐	___	_____
Color Blindness	☐	___	_____
Diabetes	☐	___	_____
Gout	☐	___	_____
Heart Problems	☐	___	_____
Hemophilia	☐	___	_____
Hypertension (High Blood Pressure)	☐	___	_____
Hysterectomy	☐	___	_____
Leukemia	☐	___	_____
Mastectomy	☐	___	_____
Mental or Emotional Problem	☐	___	_____
Prostate Trouble	☐	___	_____
Sickle Cell Anemia	☐	___	_____
Stroke	☐	___	_____
Tay-Sachs Gene	☐	___	_____

VISION

	Check	Age	Result
Myopia (nearsighted)	☐	___	_____
Hyperopia (farsighted)	☐	___	_____
Astigmatism	☐	___	_____
Presbyopia (inability to focus near)	☐	___	_____

PHYSICAL DISABILITIES (list)
_____ Age ___
_____
_____

MAJOR ILLNESSES (list)
_____ Age ___
_____
_____

Aunts only:
Age at Puberty _____
Age at Menopause _____

173

PATERNAL SIBLING (Father's Brother or Sister)

Name _____

Street Address _____ Phone _____ Business Phone _____

Date of Birth ___/___/___ Place of Birth: City _____ Apt. No. _____ City _____ State _____ State _____ ZIP _____ Country _____

If deceased, Date of Death ___/___/___ Cause of Death: _____

MEDICAL HISTORY

	Check	Age	Result
Alcohol or Drug Problem	☐		
Allergies (list)	☐		
	☐		
	☐		
Asthma	☐		
Cancer	☐		
Color Blindness	☐		
Diabetes	☐		
Gout	☐		
Heart Problems	☐		
Hemophilia	☐		
Hypertension (High Blood Pressure)	☐		
Hysterectomy	☐		
Leukemia	☐		
Mastectomy	☐		
Mental or Emotional Problem	☐		
Prostate Trouble	☐		
Sickle Cell Anemia	☐		
Stroke	☐		
Tay-Sachs Gene	☐		
Ulcers	☐		
Varicose Veins	☐		
Other (list)	☐		
	☐		

VISION

	Check	Age
Myopia (nearsighted)	☐	
Hyperopia (farsighted)	☐	
Astigmatism	☐	
Presbyopia (inability to focus near)	☐	

PHYSICAL DISABILITIES (list)

_____
_____

MAJOR ILLNESSES (list)

_____
_____

Aunts only:
Age at Puberty _____
Age at Menopause _____

174

PATERNAL SIBLING (Father's Brother or Sister)

Name _____

Street Address _____ Apt. No. _____ City _____ Phone _____ Business Phone _____

Date of Birth ___/___/___ Place of Birth: City _____ State _____ State _____ ZIP _____

If deceased, Date of Death ___/___/___ Cause of Death: _____ Country _____

MEDICAL HISTORY

	Check	Age	Result
Alcohol or Drug Problem	☐	_____	_____
Allergies (list)			
_____	☐	_____	_____
_____	☐	_____	_____
_____	☐	_____	_____
Asthma	☐	_____	_____
Cancer	☐	_____	_____
Color Blindness	☐	_____	_____
Diabetes	☐	_____	_____
Gout	☐	_____	_____
Heart Problems	☐	_____	_____
Hemophilia	☐	_____	_____
Hypertension (High Blood Pressure)	☐	_____	_____
Hysterectomy	☐	_____	_____
Leukemia	☐	_____	_____
Mastectomy	☐	_____	_____
Mental or Emotional Problem	☐	_____	_____
Prostate Trouble	☐	_____	_____
Sickle Cell Anemia	☐	_____	_____
Stroke	☐	_____	_____
Tay-Sachs Gene	☐	_____	_____

VISION

	Check	Age	Result
Myopia (nearsighted)	☐	_____	_____
Hyperopia (farsighted)	☐	_____	_____
Astigmatism	☐	_____	_____
Presbyopia (inability to focus near)	☐	_____	_____

PHYSICAL DISABILITIES (list)

	Check	Age
_____	☐	_____
_____	☐	_____
_____	☐	_____

MAJOR ILLNESSES (list)

	Check	Age
_____	☐	_____
_____	☐	_____
_____	☐	_____

Aunts only:
Age at Puberty _____
Age at Menopause _____

PHYSICIAN RECORD

It is important to keep a record of doctors regularly treating each person in the family so medical records can be transferred or recovered later. Because many doctors destroy inactive records after a certain number of years, it is wise to request records be transferred to new doctors whenever a change (for any reason) is made in physicians.

Doctor _____ Phone _____

Street Address _____ Emergency Phone _____

City _____ State _____ ZIP _____

Date started _____ Date ended _____

Doctor _____ Phone _____

Street Address _____ Emergency Phone _____

City _____ State _____ ZIP _____

Date started _____ Date ended _____

Doctor _____ Phone _____

Street Address _____ Emergency Phone _____

City _____ State _____ ZIP _____

Date started _____ Date ended _____

Doctor _____ Phone _____

Street Address _____ Emergency Phone _____

City _____ State _____ ZIP _____

Date started _____ Date ended _____

Doctor _____ Phone _____

Street Address _____ Emergency Phone _____

City _____ State _____ ZIP _____

Date started _____ Date ended _____

Doctor _____ Phone _____

Street Address _____ Emergency Phone _____

City _____ State _____ ZIP _____

Date started _____ Date ended _____

Doctor _____ Phone _____

Street Address _____ Emergency Phone _____

City _____ State _____ ZIP _____

Date started _____ Date ended _____

Doctor _____ Phone _____

Street Address _____ Emergency Phone _____

City _____ State _____ ZIP _____

Date started _____ Date ended _____

Doctor _____ Phone _____

Street Address _____ Emergency Phone _____

City _____ State _____ ZIP _____

Date started _____ Date ended _____

Doctor _____ Phone _____

Street Address _____ Emergency Phone _____

City _____ State _____ ZIP _____

Date started _____ Date ended _____

Doctor _____ Phone _____

Street Address _____ Emergency Phone _____

City _____ State _____ ZIP _____

Date started _____ Date ended _____

Doctor _____ Phone _____

Street Address _____ Emergency Phone _____

City _____ State _____ ZIP _____

Date started _____ Date ended _____

Dentist _____ Phone _____

Street Address _____ Emergency Phone _____

City _____ State _____ ZIP _____

Date started _____ Date ended _____

Dentist _____ Phone _____

Street Address _____ Emergency Phone _____

City _____ State _____ ZIP _____

Date started _____ Date ended _____

Dentist _____ Phone _____

Street Address _____ Emergency Phone _____

City _____ State _____ ZIP _____

Date started _____ Date ended _____

Dentist _____ Phone _____

Street Address _____ Emergency Phone _____

City _____ State _____ ZIP _____

Date started _____ Date ended _____

Dentist _____ Phone _____

Street Address _____ Emergency Phone _____

City _____ State _____ ZIP _____

Date started _____ Date ended _____

Dentist _____ Phone _____

Street Address _____ Emergency Phone _____

City _____ State _____ ZIP _____

Date started _____ Date ended _____

Dentist _____ Phone _____

Street Address _____ Emergency Phone _____

City _____ State _____ ZIP _____

Date started _____ Date ended _____

Dentist _____ Phone _____

Street Address _____ Emergency Phone _____

City _____ State _____ ZIP _____

Date started _____ Date ended _____

Dentist _____ Phone _____

Street Address _____ Emergency Phone _____

City _____ State _____ ZIP _____

Date started _____ Date ended _____

Dentist _____ Phone _____

Street Address _____ Emergency Phone _____

City _____ State _____ ZIP _____

Date started _____ Date ended _____

Dentist _____ Phone _____

Street Address _____ Emergency Phone _____

City _____ State _____ ZIP _____

Date started _____ Date ended _____

Dentist _____ Phone _____

Street Address _____ Emergency Phone _____

City _____ State _____ ZIP _____

Date started _____ Date ended _____

Specialist _____ Phone _____

Type of Specialty _____ Emergency Phone _____

Street Address _____ City _____ State _____ ZIP _____

Date started _____ Date ended _____

Specialist _____ Phone _____

Type of Specialty _____ Emergency Phone _____

Street Address _____ City _____ State _____ ZIP _____

Date started _____ Date ended _____

Specialist _____ Phone _____

Type of Specialty _____ Emergency Phone _____

Street Address _____ City _____ State _____ ZIP _____

Date started _____ Date ended _____

Specialist _____ Phone _____

Type of Specialty _____ Emergency Phone _____

Street Address _____ City _____ State _____ ZIP _____

Date started _____ Date ended _____

Specialist _____ Phone _____

Type of Specialty _____ Emergency Phone _____

Street Address _____ City _____ State _____ ZIP _____

Date started _____ Date ended _____

Specialist _____ Phone _____

Type of Specialty _____ Emergency Phone _____

Street Address _____ City _____ State _____ ZIP _____

Date started _____ Date ended _____

Specialist _____ Phone _____

Type of Specialty _____ Emergency Phone _____

Street Address _____ City _____ State _____ ZIP _____

Date started _____ Date ended _____

Specialist _____ Phone _____

Type of Specialty _____ Emergency Phone _____

Street Address _____ City _____ State _____ ZIP _____

Date started _____ Date ended _____

Specialist _____ Phone _____

Type of Specialty _____ Emergency Phone _____

Street Address _____ City _____ State _____ ZIP _____

Date started _____ Date ended _____

Specialist _____ Phone _____

Type of Specialty _____ Emergency Phone _____

Street Address _____ City _____ State _____ ZIP _____

Date started _____ Date ended _____

Specialist _____ Phone _____

Type of Specialty _____ Emergency Phone _____

Street Address _____ City _____ State _____ ZIP _____

Date started _____ Date ended _____

Specialist _____ Phone _____

Type of Specialty _____ Emergency Phone _____

Street Address _____ City _____ State _____ ZIP _____

Date started _____ Date ended _____